ARTFUL HANDMADE
WRAP BRACELETS

ARTFUL HANDMADE WRAP BRACELETS

Di Kim

Race Point
PUBLISHING

Race Point
PUBLISHING

A division of Book Sales, Inc.
276 Fifth Avenue Suite 206
New York, New York 10001

RACE POINT PUBLISHING and the distinctive Race Point Publishing logo
are trademarks of Book Sales, Inc.

© 2014 by Quantum Publishing Limited

This 2014 edition published by Race Point Publishing by arrangement with
Quantum Publishing Limited

This book was conceived, designed, and produced by
Quantum Publishing Limited
6 Blundell Street
London N7 9BH
United Kingdom

EDITOR Corinne Masciocchi
DESIGNER Blanche Williams at Harper Williams Ltd
PHOTOGRAPHER Nathalie Bearden

ISBN: 978-1-937994-36-5
Printed in China
2 4 6 8 10 9 7 5 3 1

www.racepointpub.com

Contents

Introduction

Friendship bracelets have come a long way since they first originated as an eighties fashion trend for teenagers. Whipping up colorfully patterned braids and exchanging them with friends were trademark characteristics of this raging jewelry fad for young girls. Like most iconic fashion trends, friendship bracelets have found their way back into today's pop culture, making colorful statements all across the world.

While the same fundamental techniques of macramé and cord knotting are still applied today, this generation's version has definitely evolved with progress, delivering a more modernized look that even includes a name change! From "friendship" to "stackable", this jewelry trend focuses on the layered look, a popular fashion style that encompasses wearing multiple pieces together at the same time. Unlike the original, today's version comes in a variety of different designs to reflect any fashion style, for any woman or man, girl or boy. Whether your sense of style expresses an eclectic boho-chic, dainty minimalism, edgy urban rock, or classic conservative, stackable jewelry is versatile enough to be worn every day.

And while the concept of layering multiple items can be applied to most apparel and jewelry, when it comes to bracelets in particular, the idea takes on a whole new meaning. Enter the global phenomenon: "Arm Candy". Over the past two years or so, the Arm Candy trend has taken over the minds (and wrists!) of young and old alike. Stemming from the layered look, Arm Candy (also known as Arm Party or Wrist Party) simply describes the collective result of stacking and layering multiple bracelets and other wrist wear (including watches) together. The name refers to the bright splashes of color from each bracelet's beads, cords, and other materials that possess a familiar resemblance to those sugary sweets we all know and love. But no matter what they're called—from friendship bracelets to stackable jewelry to that delectable Arm Candy—they all essentially go hand in hand to become a fun way for you to express your individuality. With just a few basic materials and a touch of inspiration, it's easy to create and customize pieces that reflect your own personal look and style.

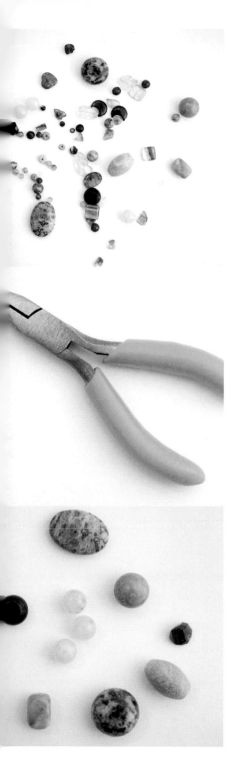

Getting started

Before you dive in with excitement and enthusiasm to create your handmade pieces, there are a few essential things you need to prepare and equip yourself with. For starters, you'll need to acquire all the necessary tools, materials, and equipment that each project requires. In bracelet-making, the basic design format consists of stringing materials, such as cords and thread, and then your focal components, like beads, charms, or links, which become the centerpiece of your jewelry. With a vast selection of jewelry supplies available, there's no limit to what you can create, even when on a budget!

Once you familiarize yourself with the materials, the next process (and the most important!) entails learning the hands-on techniques, from cord-knotting and macramé, to basic wire-wrapping and metalwork. When it comes to making cord bracelets, knowledge of basic cord braiding is a must. The two main techniques used throughout these projects include the simple three-stranded braid and the square-knot macramé. And if you know how to braid hair, then you've already got one out of two covered! All that remains is learning how to fasten and close your pieces, plus minimal use of metalwork, like incorporating jewelry wire, jump rings, and other findings. Although it may seem like a lot to keep track of and learn, try not to let yourself get overwhelmed. It's best to take things slowly, at your own pace, and always with an open mind. Take all the time you need, rather than rush through in haste, make a mistake, and end up having to go back and relearn everything. Read all the steps thoroughly to ensure full knowledge and understanding—it's definitely worth it! By learning just a few of the techniques, you'll uncover a whole new world of creating beautiful jewelry.

Materials and tools

Everything you'll need to start building bracelets falls into three catagories: stringing materials, which are used as the base of a design to hold your choice of embellishment or bead; beads and findings, which are the bulk and main technical aspect of the design; and tools—the essential equipment needed to build your project.

Thread

Stringing materials

Your choice of stringing material greatly determines the final look and design of your jewelry project, and with so many types to choose from, it's easy to create pieces that reflect your personal taste or style, and even meet your budget. Most stringing material can be categorized into beading threads, cords, or jewelry wire.

Threads and cords are most often used for bead stringing, and come in a variety of fibers—from cotton and waxed linen, to silk and ribbon. Cotton embroidery floss

and knotting cords are most commonly used with weaving and braiding techniques since cotton is readily available at a very low price. Silk cords are integrated with pearl beads through a technique known as pearl knotting. However, working with silk cords can be tricky at times—its soft, silky texture makes for a slippery surface and fray very easily.

Selecting the right size thread or cord for your beads is also a factor to consider, as it will be determined mainly by the size of the bead hole. Fortunately, most threads and cords come in different thicknesses (measured in millimeters), to accommodate your jewelry components. Nearly all the projects in this book work with 1mm thread or cord, as it fits standard bead sizes. Finally, the best part is choosing your cord or thread colors.

Leather and suede are alternative stringing materials to incorporate into your jewelry designs to bring a natural element and texture. But leather is easier to work with than suede, and as a result, is used more often. Leather stringing materials can be

Cords

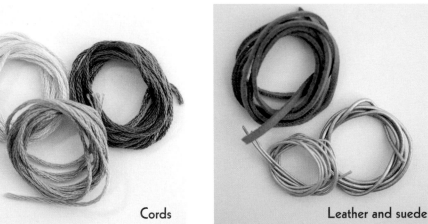

Leather and suede

...und in a variety of sizes and in two basic ...rms: round or flat cords. The latter is ...ommonly referred to as "calf lace", as the ...rds are usually made using calfskin hide. ...oth types of leather cord are also available ... several color options, but selection at ...mes can be rather minimal due to the ...ngthy and complicated dye process.

...ewelry (or beading) wire is almost always ...ade from metal and can be used to add ... different element to your project in the ...rm of wirework. Wire also allows more ...ays in which to incorporate beads into ...ewelry by applying a technique called ...ire-wrapping. Simple loops or eye pins ...an be made through basic wire-wrapping, ...hile more complex wrapping techniques ...an allow you to make your own metal ...ewelry findings, components, or clasps. ...eading wire can be found in four basic ...etal colors—gold, silver, copper, and ...rass—although aluminum wire in particular ... offered in a rainbow of metallic colors. ...ike cords and thread, jewelry wire also ...omes in different sizes and widths,

measured in gauges—the higher the number, the thinner the wire. For general wire-wrapping, the most ideal size to use is 24 gauge, as the wire needs to be thick and strong enough to hold most components, yet thin and pliable to withstand twisting and bending without breaking. Characteristically, metal tends to get harder when restructuring its shape (or molecular bond): in other words, the more you keep bending the same piece of wire over and over, the stiffer and less malleable it gets, until the wire eventually breaks. Sterling silver and 14-karat gold-filled wire is also offered in two different measures of malleability: half-hard and dead-soft. As the name suggests, dead-soft wire is the most malleable, meaning it can withstand more bends. It is best for more complicated wire-wrapping that entails multiple loops and turns, while half-hard wire is sufficient enough for basic loops and wraps.

Beads and findings

Once you've determined the foundation of your design, comes the fun part of

embellishing it! There are hundreds of jewelry-making components to choose from, broken down into two main categories: beads and jewelry findings.

Glass seed beads come in a plethora of colors and finishes. Seed bead sizes are shown with two numbers separated by a forward slash—for instance, "8/0". The first number indicates the number of beads, lined up in a row, that is equivalent to 1in (2.5cm), so here, eight beads lined up is equal to 1in (2.5cm) in length. Size 12/0 seed beads means that 12 beads lined up is equal to 1in (2.5cm) in length, and so on. The higher the number, the smaller the size of the seed bead. Other beads, like gemstones, crystals, and metal are sized by diameter in millimeters.

Crystal beads possess a brighter polish and shine than glass beads, making them very appealing. Although crystal is a form of glass, the process of making it results in a superior finish, putting crystal in its own separate category. The Austrian-based

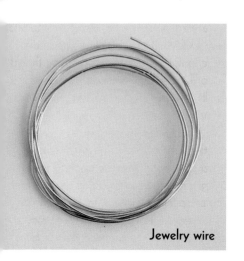

Jewelry wire

Glass seed beads

Crystal beads

Metal beads

Semiprecious beads

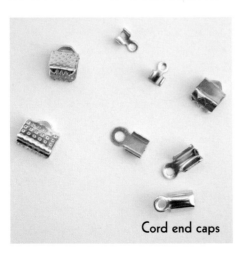
Cord end caps

company, Swarovski Elements, is renowned worldwide for crystal-making, and has been unrivaled for many years. As always, cheaper imitations are available, but you simply won't get the same sparkle and brilliance of Swarovski.

Metal beads can usually be found in the form of precious metals (i.e. sterling silver, 14-karat gold-filled) and non-precious metals (i.e. pewter, brass, or copper). However, with the cost of precious metals being rather high, a cheaper option is available in the form of plated metal beads. A non-precious metal, such as brass, is used as the base of a component, and is then dipped or plated with a layer of either silver or gold to look like the real thing. The downside to using this cheaper alternative results in the gold or silver layer chipping away overtime to expose the base metal underneath. Although the decision to use real or plated beads is up to you, it's worth spending a little more money on precious metal beads to make your creations last a lifetime.

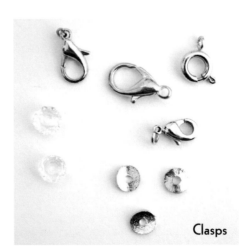
Clasps

Semiprecious beads are made up of any naturally mined stone or mineral found on Earth. Gemstone beads tend to cost more than any crystal, glass, or plated metal bead because of the process it takes to create them. The most popular and commonly used gemstones include quartz, like amethyst and citrine, turquoise, topaz, opal, jade, garnet, and agate.

Findings, unlike beads, cover a broad range of components that all differ in use. For example, jump rings, cord end caps, head pins, and eye pins all serve to connect one component to another and are not the main attraction. Jump rings are made with either open or closed seams. The latter entails a continuous loop as a result of soldering together cut seams of an open jump ring. Cord end caps come in a variety of types to fit different cords or threads. Most common are foldover end caps, where tiny prongs are pinched down on top of the cord to hold it in place. Head and eye pins are a type of jewelry wire used to hold beads or pendants that are affixed to a base finding, such as chains or earring hoops. Head pins possess a flat end, similar to a nail head, where pendants or charms are strung onto the wire to rest on top of the head. On the other side sits an open loop that is used for attachment. Eye pins have two open loops on either side to use for linking components together.

Most jewelry findings are made of metal, from sterling silver and gold-filled, to brass and pewter. No matter the embellishment you choose, always expect a bit of trial and error when working with the different

...aterial types. As you begin working with ...ch kind of material or component, you'll ...arn what can or can't be done with certain ...nes, and you'll become familiar with their ...atures and characteristics.

...ools and equipment

...ll jewelry-making requires a set of tools ...r cutting, attaching, or gluing pieces and ...omponents together. Fortunately, because ...e projects and techniques in this book ...quire minimal skill, the tools needed are ...asic and can easily be found at any local ...obby or craft shop.

A **ruler** is essential, whether it's to measure ...e length of a cord or the diameter of a ...ead. It's good to obtain a ruler with both ...etric (millimeters and centimeters) and ...mperial (inches) units of measurement. ...or ease of use, the projects in this book ...nclude both units.

Thread glue is almost always applied to ...he tips of cut thread, otherwise the thread ...vill most likely fray or unravel. Most thread ...lue (sometimes referred to as beading ...lue) can be found at any local craft and ...obby store. Alternatively, clear nail polish ...lso works well as an adhesive for cotton, ...ilk, or any fiber. General all-purpose glue ...vill sometimes do the job, so long as the ...adhesive is permanent and can be used on ...abric. Do not substitute with super glue, as ...t can cause skin irritation.

Pliers and wire cutters are used in projects ...that require basic metalwork. Round-nose ...pliers are used for wire-wrapping—as the ...name suggests, these pliers have cylindrical-shaped noses to make perfect round circles by wrapping the wire around the nose in a loop.

Chain-nose pliers are your all-purpose, go-to pliers. Their flattened noses make it easy to grip, hold, pull, squeeze, tighten, or loosen almost anything. It's important not to confuse chain-nose pliers with flat-nose pliers (designed with rows of jagged teeth lining the jaws) as the sharp, uneven edges will scratch and damage your components. Finally, wire cutters are used for cutting metal, mostly wire and chain.

Once you've acquired all the necessary tools and materials, you'll need a good workspace, like a desk or table, to spread everything out and make your supplies easily accessible while working. It's also important to have a flat surface to secure your cords to while braiding, using sticky tape to hold them down. A clipboard or anything with a flat base will work just fine as well.

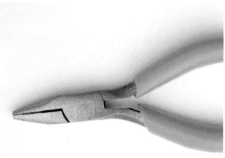

Clear nail polish and thread glue

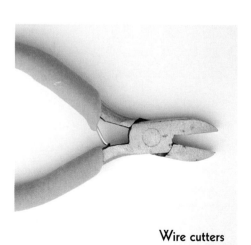

Wire cutters

Chain-nose pliers

Round-nose pliers

Basic braids and knots

The three-stranded braid and the square-knot macramé techniques are two of the most basic weave patterns that both require a minimal level of skill. While reading and learning the steps below, you may discover that you already know how to perform them!

Three-stranded braid

The three-stranded braid is the most basic and commonly used weave. It's also the easiest braid to learn and is applied frequently in hair styling and jewelry-making. In jewelry, your choice of materials to use is unlimited. Leather or cotton cords, embroidery thread, and ribbon are just some examples. In addition, various jewelry findings and beads can be incorporated to enhance the design. With an endless supply of materials, many find that the most difficult process is not making the piece, but selecting which components to use!

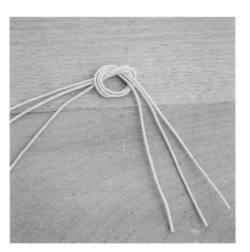

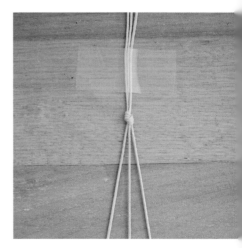

1 Cut your choice of cord into three strands, each measuring 12in (30cm).

2 Align the tips of all three strands and tie an overhand knot 3in (7.5cm) from one end.

3 Secure the strands onto a clipboard by taping down the 3in (7.5cm) end of the cords. Separate each of the longer strands by lining them up next to each other.

4 Take the outer-left cord and lay it over the center cord. The left cord is now the center cord.

5 Next take the outer-right cord and place it over the current center cord.

TIP

Your braid can be as tight or as loose as you prefer, but make sure that the strands are even and not lopsided, as an uneven pull will cause unsightly kinks and lumps in the braid.

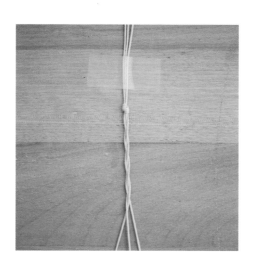

6 Repeat Steps 4 and 5, alternating between left and right cords, and placing each one over the center cord as you go.

7 Once you reach the desired length, tie another overhand knot to secure the braid and prevent it from unraveling. Congratulations! You've just completed the three-stranded braiding technique!

Square-knot macramé

In the art of macramé, the square knot is most commonly used. Often times, it is the only knot used, particularly in jewelry-making. It comprises two half knots made in reverse of the other, or a right-handed overhand knot and a left-handed overhand knot simply repeated over and over until reaching the desired length. The set-up of this braiding method requires two separate sets of cords: base cords and tying cords. The base cords act as the center spine of the macramé bracelet, while the tying cords are used to make the square knots around the stationary base cords. The best types of cords to use for square-knot macramé braiding are cotton, waxed linen, or knotting cords.

1 Cut your choice of cord into three strands: one measuring 15in (38cm) and two measuring 3ft (91cm).

2 Align the tips of all three strands and tie an overhand knot about 3in (7.5cm) from the end.

TIP

While braiding the square-knot macramé, keep the following phrase in mind as a helpful reminder: OVER, OVER, UNDER—1st half knot UNDER, UNDER, OVER—2nd half knot.

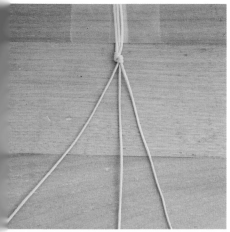

TIP

Make sure you always complete a full square knot before stopping or adding any beads or components—this will help you keep track of which half knot you left off from. Repeating the same half knot twice in a row will cause an uneven bump/twist in the braid.

Secure the strands onto a clipboard by taping down the 3in (7.5cm) end of the cords. Arrange the cords so that the shortest cord (the base cord) is in between the two longer ones (the tying cords).

4 Take the left tying cord and place it OVER the base cord, crossing it to the right side. Both tying cords should now be to the right of the base cord.

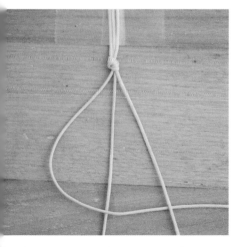

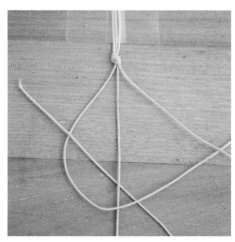

5 Next place the right tying cord OVER (or on top of) the left tying cord, and then bring it UNDER the base cord across to the other side.

6 Then pull the right tying cord through the loop on the left side made by the left tying cord and pull both cords at the same time to tighten the knot around the base cord.

You have completed the first half of the square knot. (Note that both tying cords have switched places: the original left tying cord became the right, and vice versa.)

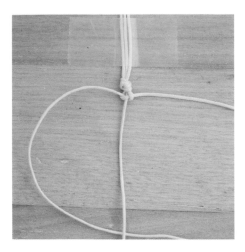

7 For the second half of the square knot, take the left tying cord and place it UNDER the base cord, crossing it to the right side.

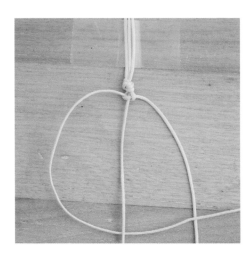

8 With both tying cords on the right side again, place the right tying cord UNDER the left one, and then bring it OVER the base cord across to the other side.

9 Pull the right tying cord through the loop on the left and pull both cords at the same time to tighten the knot around the base cord.

You have just completed one full square knot. (Note that both tying cords have returned to their original starting places.)

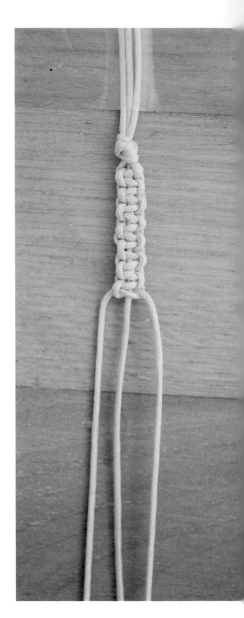

10 To finish a macramé braid, repeat Steps 4–9 to continue making full square knots until you reach the desired length.

Fastenings

Cord bracelets use two main fastening methods: adjustable or non-adjustable closures. To re-size a bracelet, allow extra cord if needed, then bead or braid until you've reached your desired length. If the bracelet features a centerpiece, add half of the desired extra length to the first half of the bracelet, and half to the second half, after the centerpiece has been placed.

Adjustable pull-tie closures

An adjustable bracelet uses a pull-tie closure, where the loose ends on each side of the bracelet cross and overlap to form a circle. Their intersecting point is then held together by a braid, knot, or bead that slides along both end ties. The bracelet can be tightened by pulling on both end ties or loosened by pulling them apart.

TIP

The overlap should measure only about 4in (10cm) and the sticky tape should be placed toward the top of the overlap so that the rest of the section provides room to make the sliding braid.

1 Cut a 7in (18cm) piece of matching cord that was used to make the bracelet.

2 Take both loose ends of the bracelet and overlap them to form a circle, with each end going in the opposite direction of the other.

3 While still holding that shape, secure the bracelet to a clipboard by taping down part of the overlapped section, with the loose ends placed vertically. These will be the base cords.

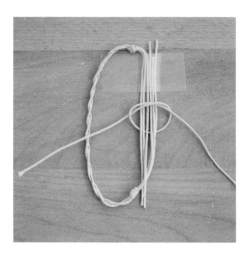

4 Take the 7in (18cm) strand of cord by the center and place it perpendicularly underneath the base cords. Then tie an

overhand knot around the base cords. The loose ends of the 7in (18cm) cord will be the tying cords.

5 Make a ¼in (6mm) macramé braid, or three full square knots (see pp.16–18).

6 Tie an overhand knot with the tying cords and cut the excess strands. Dab thread glue or clear nail polish to secure the knot and keep it from coming undone.

7 Then tie an overhand knot on each loose end of the bracelet and trim any excess strands. The knots at the end of the ties will act as stoppers to prevent the cords from being pulled all the way off the sliding braid.

8 Test out the pull-tie closure by pulling the end ties back and forth apart.

Non-adjustable bead closures

Non-adjustable bracelets secure through button bead closures hooked on by a loop, or with metal clasps that fasten on to a small ring or loop either end of the piece. While non-adjustable pieces lack the characteristic that allow them to fit a wide range of wrist sizes, this feature does provide wearers with the option of customizing bracelets to their preferred comfort and fit. The non-adjustable bracelets in this book are built to a standard length of 7in (18cm), and should fit snugly around your wrist, as they will stretch with wear.

1 Cut the length and quantity of cord strands, as per specific project instructions. Align the tips of all cords on one side.

2 Secure the cords to a clipboard by taping down 4in (10cm) from the end, so that the even ends point down. Using the three-stranded braid technique (see pp.14–15), make a braid 1in (2.5cm) long.

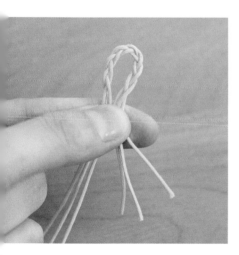

3 Remove the cords from the clipboard and fold the braid in half. Tie an overhand knot with the doubled-up cord strands. Before tightening the knot completely, make sure the loop is the correct size to fit the button bead it will accommodate.

4 Trim the excess strands from the ends that were just braided, not the longer cord strands that will be used to make the bracelet. Dab thread glue or clear nail polish to secure the knot.

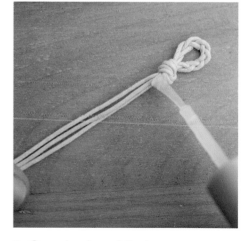

5 Once the glue is fully dry, return to the project steps to complete the bracelet. Afterwards, follow instructions on securing the bead button, as provided within each project.

The projects

Stackable bracelets have quickly gained popularity within the world of fashion accessories, and it's easy to understand how and why! This unique trend creates an opportunity for wearers to express their own individual sense of style by stacking and layering multiple pieces at the same time. To get you started, here is a gallery of bracelets to build—and any one can be modified to your taste. From cords and strings to beads and chains, there's an endless number of options available to start mixing, matching, and building your stack. Use your inspiration and imagination to create jewelry that is truly yours—feel free to substitute a cord color (or even a bead!) that's more to your taste and liking. To truly personalize your collection, give each bracelet a fun and flirty name that captures its best qualities. And most importantly, have fun!

Precious metals

Metal jewelry brings a timeless elegance that never goes out of style and complements any component with classic sophistication. Metal comes in a variety of forms, but only a dozen or so are used for jewelry-making. While sterling silver and 14-karat gold are more popular and preferred, their rarity makes them highly valuable and extremely costly. More abundant and readily available are non-precious metals, such as aluminum, iron, copper, bronze, and zinc. Many beads and findings are made using a non-precious metal for the base and then dipped or plated in genuine silver or gold. These plated components are an easy alternative to the real thing at a fraction of the price.

Natalie

SIZE: 7in (18cm) bracelet

Defined with an elegant simplicity and a clean silhouette, this sleek piece features a long, curved gold metal tube bead strung onto braided cotton cords in a deep purple hue, for a modern and minimal look that still makes a statement. A simple loop hooks onto a dainty gold button bead to finish off and secure the bracelet. This dainty bracelet is a must-have for those with a minimalist fashion style.

TOOLS AND MATERIALS

- 1mm cotton embroidery thread in purple
- Ruler
- Scissors
- Thread glue (or clear nail polish)
- Clipboard
- Sticky tape
- 2mm x 20mm gold-plated curved tube bar
- 6mm gold disc button bead

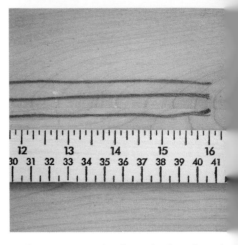

1 Cut three strands of purple thread, each measuring about 16in (40.5cm).

2 Line up the ends of all three cords and make a braided loop for the button bead closure (see p.21). Make sure the loop is slightly larger than the disc button bead—in this case, the loop should be about 3/8in (8–10mm). Trim any excess thread.

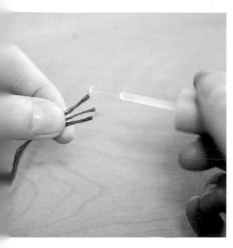

Dab the other ends of the cords with thread glue or clear nail polish. Leave the glue to dry. The stiffened, glued ends will make it easier to thread the tube bar onto the cords and prevent the ends from fraying.

4 Secure the cords to the clipboard by taping down the button loop.

5 Separate each strand and begin making a tight braid using the three-stranded braid technique (see pp.14–15). Continue until the braid measures 7in (18cm).

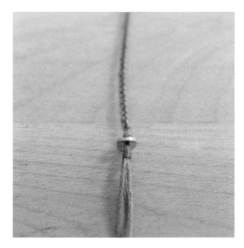

Remove the braided cords from the clipboard. String on the gold tube bar by bunching all three strands together and sliding them through the bar to the center of the braid.

7 Tie an overhand knot after 6in (15cm) of braid, then string on the gold disc button bead.

8 Finish with another overhand knot, trim the excess cord, and dab the knot with thread glue or clear nail polish to keep it from unraveling.

Blanche

SIZE: 7in (18cm) bracelet

Deceptively simple in design, this bracelet features the three-stranded braid, only this time, a very fine and delicate silver chain partners with one of the three strands to create this sophisticated, classic look. The soft and subtle hue of the cream-colored cord becomes the perfect backdrop for the bright silver chain, producing tiny brilliant sparkles of silver light that glisten from your wrist.

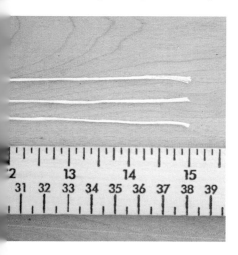

TOOLS AND MATERIALS

- 1mm cotton embroidery thread in cream
- Ruler
- Scissors
- 6mm silver disc bead button
- Thread glue (or clear nail polish)
- 1.5mm silver light cable chain
- Wire cutters
- Clipboard
- Sticky tape

1 Cut three strands of the cream-colored thread, each measuring about 16in (40.5cm).

2 Line up the ends of all three cords and make a braided loop for the button bead closure (see p.21). Make sure the loop is slightly larger than the disc button bead—in this case, the loop should be about 3/8in (8–10mm). Trim any excess thread.

3 Dab the other ends of the cords with thread glue or clear nail polish. Leave the glue to dry. The stiffened, glued ends will prevent the cords from fraying as well as make it easier to string on the chain link.

4 While waiting for the glue to dry, measure the silver chain at 6½in (16.5cm), and cut the chain link that falls at the measured mark using wire cutters.

5 Separate each strand and thread the outer-left strand through the end link of the silver chain. Bring the link all the way up until it sits next to the knot at the button loop.

TIP
....
When tying the overhand knot used to secure the chain to the cord, be sure the knot sits very close to the bottom of the braided loop, otherwise there will be a small portion in the beginning of the braid without the chain component.

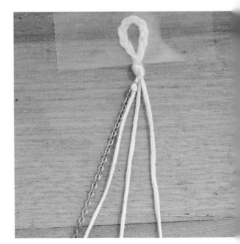

6 Secure the chain link in place by tying an overhand knot with only the outer-left cord that holds the chain. This specific cord and chain will be used together as one strand during braiding.

7 Secure the strands to the clipboard by taping down the button loop. You should have four strands: three cotton cords and one silver chain.

Begin braiding the cords and chain using the three-stranded braid technique (see pp.14–15). Continue until all of the chain has been braided with the cords.

9 Tie an overhand knot with all three cotton cords to close off the braid.

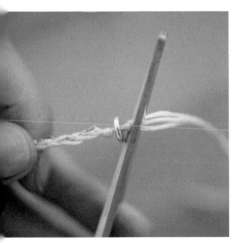

10 String on the silver disc bead and finish with another overhand knot. Remember to trim off the excess cords and dab the end knot with thread glue or clear nail polish to keep it from coming undone.

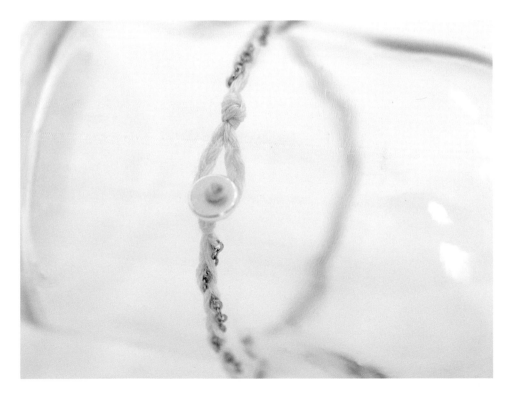

Meryl

SIZE: Adjustable, one size fits most

Follow the trend of stackable Arm Candy with this simple and timeless design. Chunky gold nugget beads are the centerpiece between woven macramé braids in a soft, subtle ash gray. These little nuggets possess facets where the beads have been cut or sliced, yielding a flat surface that results in enhanced sparkle and shine. Originally made of a sterling-silver base, these metal beads are then dipped in a 14-karat metallic gold finish—a particular type of metal plating more commonly known as "vermeil". But regardless of the process, the end result creates a versatile piece that can be worn with everything—it's the perfect stacking bracelet!

TOOLS AND MATERIALS

- 1mm cotton embroidery thread in light gray
- Ruler
- Scissors
- Thread glue (or clear nail polish)
- Seven 5mm gold-plated (vermeil) faceted nugget beads
- Clipboard
- Sticky tape

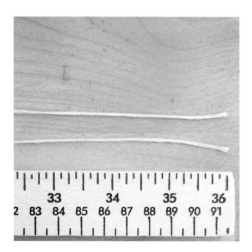

1 Cut five lengths of thread: two lengths measuring 15in (38cm), two lengths measuring 3ft (91cm), and one length measuring 7in (18cm).

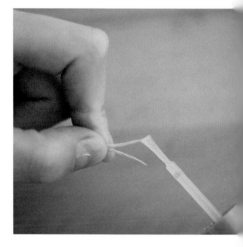

2 Apply thread glue or clear nail polish to the tips of both ends of the two 15in (38cm) cords. Leave the glue to dry. The stiffened, glued ends will make it easier to thread the beads onto the cords and prevent them from fraying.

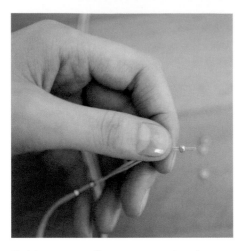

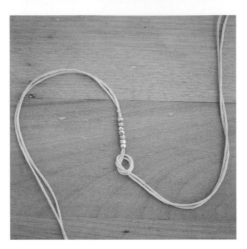

3 Next, string all seven nugget beads onto both 15in (38cm) cords—these will act as the base cords. (Using two cords instead of one will give better support, as well as help to balance out the weight of the metal beads.)

4 With the beads all lined up, position the row of beads in the center of the strands. Tie an overhand knot on either side of the beads.

5 Then secure the beaded cords to the clipboard by taping down one end.

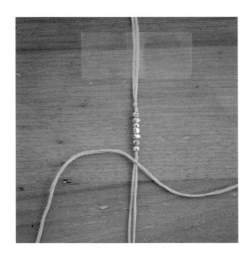

> ### TIP
> ....
> *Be sure both sides of the tying cord are approximately equal in length, otherwise you will run out of cord on one side while braiding.*

6 Take one of the 3ft (91cm) tying cords by the center and place it perpendicularly under the base cords. Tie an overhand knot around the base cords, just below the knot.

7 Using the square-knot macramé technique (see pp.16–18), make a braid about 2–3in (5–7.5cm) long.

TIP

Remember to leave about 3–4in (7.5–10cm) of loose, unbraided strands at the end, to use as pull-ties for the adjustable closure.

8 When finished, tie an overhand knot with just the tying cords. Dab thread glue on the knot to keep it from unraveling, and then trim the excess strands of the tying cord.

9 Remove the piece from the clipboard, flip it over, and tape down the other end (which is now the side with the macramé braid). Repeat Steps 6–8 with the unbraided side of the cords, using the remaining 3ft (91cm) strand.

10 Using the 7in (18cm) length of cord, make an adjustable pull-tie closure (see pp.19–20) to finish the bracelet.

Scarlett

ymbolizing love and friendship, a simple circle is the feature to this eternity bracelet
nd remains a classic favorite accessory for people of all ages. Set between woven
acramé braids in a vibrant red, this gold circle link boasts a textured finish and is
4in (2cm) wide. Its basic round shape makes this piece great for all minimalists
nd is perfect for gift-giving—a true friendship bracelet!

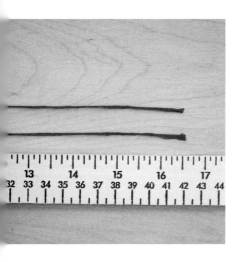

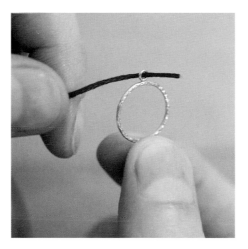

TOOLS AND MATERIALS

- 1mm cotton embroidery thread in red
- Ruler
- Scissors
- 3/4in (2cm) gold-plated circle link
  with two loops
- Clipboard
- Sticky tape
- Thread glue (or clear nail polish)

Cut five lengths of thread: two strands
easuring 15in (38cm), which will be
e base cords, two strands measuring
ft (91cm), which will be the tying cords,
nd one length measuring 7in (18cm).

2 Thread a 15in (38cm) base cord through
one of the loops on the circle link.

3 Fold the cord in half by bringing the ends together to make two strands, and then tie an overhand knot at the base of the loop.

4 Repeat Step 3 with the other side of the link using the remaining 15in (38cm) base cord.

5 Tape down one side of the loose strands to the clipboard.

6 Take one of the 3ft (91cm) tying cords by the center and place it perpendicularly under the base cords. Tie an overhand knot around the base cords, just below the loop of the circle link.

7 Using the square-knot macramé technique (see pp.16–18), make a braid 3in (7.5cm) long.

8 Close off the braid by making an overhand knot with the tying cords.

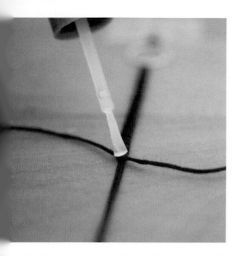

Cut the excess strands of the tying cords nd dab thread glue or clear nail polish on e knot to prevent it from unraveling.

10 Remove the cords from the clipboard, secure the other side, and repeat Steps 6–9 with the base cords on the other side of the link, using the remaining 3ft (91cm) tying cord. When finished, remove the cords from the clipboard. You should have about 4in (10cm) of loose strands on each side of a 3in (7.5cm) macramé braid, with the circle link at the center.

11 Using the 7in (18cm) length of cord, make an adjustable pull-tie closure (see pp.19–20) to finish the bracelet.

(see pp.19–20)

> ### TIP
> ....
> When cutting excess strands, try to trim the cords as close to the knot as possible to avoid any unsightly frayed threads.

Adele

SIZE: 14in (35cm) bracelet

For all those who love big, oversized accessories, this project is for you! Woven onto a double-wrapped macramé braid in gorgeous denim blue is a thick, chunky gold-plated curb chain. The pre-cut strand of chain measures approximately 2in (5cm) in length and is 8mm wide, and the flattened chain links create a dazzling shine. Stack this piece with others for a truly chunky look!

TOOLS AND MATERIALS

- 8mm gold-plated flattened curb chain
- Ruler
- Wire cutters
- 1mm cotton embroidery thread in denim blue
- Scissors
- Clipboard
- Sticky tape
- Thread glue (or clear nail polish)
- 6mm gold disc button bead

TIP

It may be necessary to apply quite a bit of force when cutting the chain with the pliers, as the hefty curb chain is significantly thicker than regular jewelry wire.

1 Measure out approximately 2in (5cm) of the flattened gold curb chain. Using wire cutters, cut the chain link that falls on the measured mark.

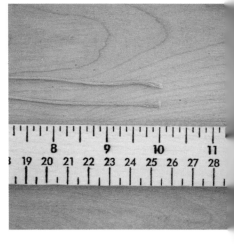

2 Cut five lengths of thread: two strands measuring 30in (76cm), two strands measuring 10in (25cm), and one strand measuring 8ft (2.45m).

3 Thread both 30in (76cm) cords onto one end of the chain links.

4 Fold the cords in half by bringing both ends of the cords together, and then tie an overhand knot onto the end link. You should have four loose strands (the base cords) hanging from the gold chain.

5 Secure the cords to the clipboard by taping down the gold chain.

6 Then take the 8ft (2.45m) strand (the tying cord) by the center and place it perpendicularly under the base cords. Tie an overhand knot around the base cords, just below the last chain link.

7 Using the square-knot macramé technique (see pp.16–18), make a braid about 12in (30cm) long.

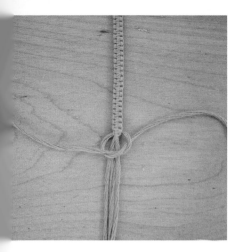

When the braid reaches the desired length, close it off by making an overhand knot with the tying cords.

9 Cut the excess strands of the tying cords and dab thread glue or clear nail polish on the knot to prevent it from unraveling.

10 String the gold disc button bead onto the base cord strands, slide it up just below the macramé braid, and close with another overhand knot. Cut off excess cords and dab thread glue on the knot. Remove the cords from the clipboard.

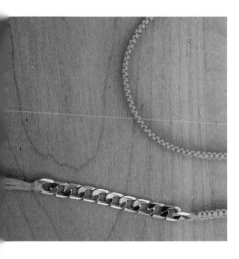

11 Thread both 10in (25cm) cords onto the other side of the chain links and fold them in half by bringing both ends of the cords together. Then tie an overhand knot at the chain link.

TIP

Since the braided loop is made using the three-stranded braid technique (see pp.14–15), and there are four cords to braid with here, two of the strands must double up as one strand while braiding.

12 With the four loose cords, make a braided loop for the button closure (see p.21), making sure the loop is slightly larger than the disc button bead—in this case, the loop should be about $^3/_8$in (8–10mm). Trim any excess thread to finish the bracelet.

Gwen

ZE: 20in (50cm) bracelet

Nothing says edgy or rock-chic better than black leather and silver metal! This multiwrap piece is simple in design and easy to create, but certainly makes a bold statement. Three large silver-plated ball beads, decorated with an engraved pattern, are strung onto a long, round black leather cord that wraps around your wrist three times—this piece is made for those who love to live loudly!

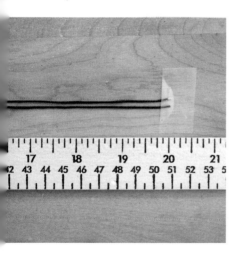

TOOLS AND MATERIALS

- 1mm black round leather cord
- Ruler
- Scissors
- Two 3mm silver-plated crimp ends
- Thread glue (or clear nail polish), optional
- Chain-nose pliers
- Three 15mm silver-plated ball beads
- Two 6mm silver-plated open jump rings
- 6mm silver-plated closed jump ring
- Silver-plated lobster clasp

1 Cut two strands of leather cord, both measuring 20in (50cm).

2 Take both cords, make sure they are aligned, and tie an overhand knot about 3in (7.5cm) from one end. Both cords will be used together as one strand, since the bead holes are large enough to accommodate two 1mm cords strung through at the same time. Plus, the doubled strands will balance out the weight of the large silver balls.

TIP
....
When folding down the crimp ends, use one hand to hold the loop ring of the crimp, placing your thumb down over the cords to keep them in place. Use your other hand to grasp the pliers.

3 Insert both cord tips on the 3in (7.5cm) side into a crimp end. If you like, you can add a drop of thread glue or clear nail polish to the cord ends for extra hold.

4 Fold and pinch down one side of the crimp end over the top of the cords using chain-nose pliers. Repeat with the other side of the crimp end.

TIP
....
Use your own preference on how the beads should be spaced—it's up to you to determine whether the beads should sit close together on the cords or have some room to slide.

5 String all three ball beads on the other side of the leather cords.

6 Tie an overhand knot with both cords on either side of the outer beads.

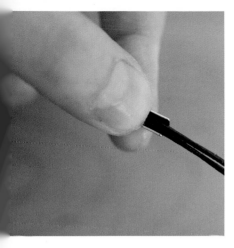

Making sure the leather cords are not twisted together, insert the other end of the cord tips into the remaining crimp end.

8 Fold and pinch down both sides of the crimp end over the cords. You should have double-stranded leather cords with crimp ends attached to either side and a row of three silver beads about 3in (7.5cm) down from one end of the cords.

9 Slip an open jump ring onto the loop of one of the crimp ends. Before closing it, slip the closed jump ring onto the open one. The closed jump ring will be the fastening loop for the lobster clasp.

10 Close the open jump ring by holding one side between your index finger and thumb, and use the chain-nose pliers to line up the seams of the ring.

11 Slip the remaining open jump ring onto the loop of the other crimp end.

12 To finish the bracelet, hook the lobster clasp onto the open jump ring and follow the instructions in Step 10 to close the ring.

Jodie

SIZE: Adjustable, one size fits most

One of the best features of cord bracelets is the ability to customize the pieces through personal color selections. But this piece takes personalized customization to another level with a neat engravable option. Suspended between dark navy blue cords is a thin, oval I.D. tag in sterling silver, and completely blank on both sides, allowing you to engrave or stamp anything from your name to an inspirational word. The possibilities are endless to make this piece truly your own!

TOOLS AND MATERIALS

- 4mm silver shade Swarovski crystal cube bead
- 1in (2.5cm) silver-plated headpin
- Chain-nose pliers
- Wire cutters
- Round-nose pliers
- 10mm silver-plated sun charm with attached jump ring
- 6x24mm sterling silver oval I.D. tag with two holes
- 1mm cotton embroidery thread in navy blue
- Ruler
- Scissors
- Thread glue (or clear nail polish)
- 5mm round silver-plated bead with 2.5mm hole

1 String the crystal cube bead onto the headpin and, using chain-nose pliers, bend the wire 90 degrees after the bead.

2 Then cut off about ¼in (6mm) of the wire tip using wire cutters.

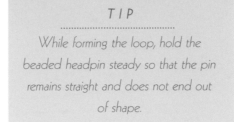

TIP

While forming the loop, hold the beaded headpin steady so that the pin remains straight and does not end out of shape.

3 Next, grasp the very tip of the bent wire with round-nose pliers, and slowly rotate the pliers inward (without letting go of the wire tip) to form a complete loop, with the tip of the wire touching the top of the crystal bead.

4 Combine the crystal and sun charm by slipping the headpin loop of the crystal charm onto the attached jump ring on the sun charm.

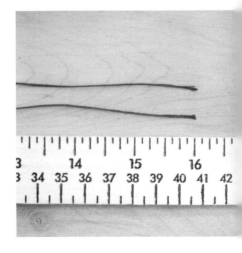

5 Before closing the jump ring, hook it onto one of the holes on the I.D. tag. Close the jump ring by holding one side between your index finger and thumb, and with the other holding the chain-nose

pliers, line up the seams of the ring. The oval link should now have a sun—crystal charm bundle dangling from one of the open holes.

6 Cut two 15in (38cm) lengths of navy blue thread.

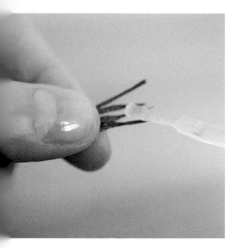

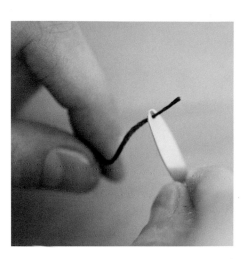

Dab all four tips with thread glue or ~~cl~~ear nail polish and leave the glue to ~~d~~ry. The stiffened, glued ends will make ~~it~~ easier to thread the cords through the ~~lin~~k or bead holes.

8 Once the glue is dry, thread a blue cord through one of the holes on the I.D. tag. Fold the cord in half by bringing both ends together and then tie an overhand knot on the link.

9 Repeat with the remaining cord on the other hole. Note that one of the holes is shared with the charm bundle. You should have two loose strands tied on each hole of the silver link.

10 Take the ends of one side of the cords ~~a~~nd thread both strands through the round ~~b~~ead. Tie an overhand knot about 2in ~~(~~5cm) from the end and trim the excess ~~s~~trands after the knot.

11 Thread the two other strands through the same bead, going in from the opposite side. Tie an overhand knot about 2in (5cm) from the end and trim excess strands. This bead pull-tie is an alternative adjustable closure and adjusts by pulling the end ties through the bead to loosen or tighten the bracelet.

Angelina

SIZE: Adjustable, one size fits most

Bold and daring, yet modern and chic—this piece possesses an urban, rock style that's both feminine and dainty at the same time. Floating across braided cotton cords in a dark charcoal gray, are seven tiny golden rings made from a brass base metal and finished with a layer of shiny gold plating. If you're looking to make an edgy statement but still want to keep a soft, girlish touch, look no further than this perfectly balanced piece!

TOOLS AND MATERIALS

- 1mm cotton embroidery thread in charcoal gray
- Ruler
- Scissors
- Thread glue (or clear nail polish)
- Clipboard
- Sticky tape
- Seven 5mm gold-plated disc rings

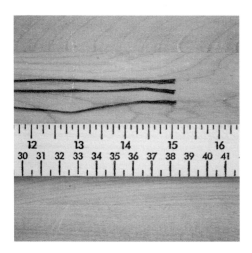

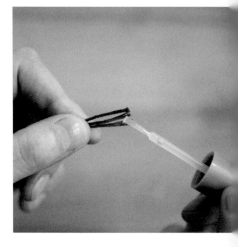

1 Cut four lengths of thread: three lengths measuring 15in (38cm) and one length measuring 7in (18cm).

2 Apply thread glue or clear nail varnish to the tips of both ends of all three 15in (38cm) cords. Leave the glue to dry. The stiffened, glued ends will make it easier to thread the rings onto the cords and prevent them from fraying.

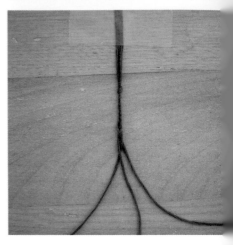

3 Align the ends and tie an overhand knot with all three cords, about 3—4in (7.5–10cm) from one end of the cords.

4 Secure the shorter side of the cords to the clipboard, and then separate each strand.

5 Using the three-stranded braid techniqu (see pp.14–15), make a tight braid about 1 (2.5cm) long.

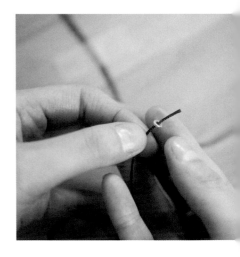

6 Next, string a disc ring onto the outer-left strand. Bring it all the way up to the bottom of the braid, and then bring this strand over the center one to keep the ring in place.

TIP
....
When adding a disc ring to the braid, make sure to hold the strands in place by pinching the end of the braid so that it does not unravel and come undone.

7 Continue braiding for ½in (1.2cm). The add another ring to the outer-left strand.

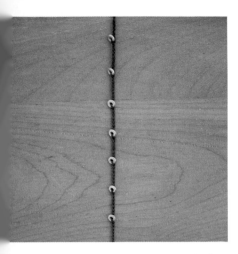

Keep repeating Steps 6 and 7 until all the rings have been braided on.

9 After adding the last ring, make a final 1in (2.5cm) braid, and then tie an overhand knot with all three cords to close off the weave. You should have seven gold rings, approximately every inch (2.5cm) along the braid, with loose, excess strands on both sides measuring between 3–4in (7.5–10cm) long.

10 Remove the cords from the clipboard. Using the 7in (18cm) length of cord, make an adjustable pull-tie closure (see pp.19–20) to finish the bracelet.

Glenn

SIZE: 7in (18cm) bracelet

This simple design features flat calfskin leather cords in a twisted braid pattern that creates a cylindrical shape. In a natural brown color tone, this piece, unlike all the others, brings no fancy sparkle or decorated embellishment to the table; however, these unpretentious qualities offer a greater versatility for wearers by making it unisex in style. And although seemingly bare and unadorned, there is one rather unique feature about this piece that sets it apart from any other—the tube-shaped magnetic clasp. This ingenious fastening mechanism allows the bracelet to be put on and taken off easily.

TOOLS AND MATERIALS

- 3mm natural brown flat leather cord
- Ruler
- Scissors
- Clipboard
- Sticky tape
- Thread glue (or clear nail polish)
- 7x16mm silver-plated magnetic clasp set

1 Cut three equal lengths of the leather cord, each measuring approximately 9in (23cm).

2 Stack the cords on top of each other, making sure all three are evenly aligned. Then tape down the ends on one side to the clipboard, with no more than 1in (2.5cm) of the ends covered.

3 Using the three-stranded braid technique (see pp.14–15), tightly braid the leather cords by rolling the strands inward when crossing over the center each time. Close, tight-knit braids will create a tubular shape with the leather, rather than a flat, linear braid. Continue with the entire length of the cords.

4 Next, tape down the bottom end of the braid to prevent it from unraveling.

5 Using a ruler, measure the braid from 0in (0cm) to 7in (18cm) and mark those spots using thread glue or clear nail polish. Apply a generous amount, covering all sides of the braid. Leave the glue to dry completely. The stiffened areas will help keep the braid's cylindrical shape when trimming the leather cords, as well as prevent the braid from unraveling.

6 Once the glue has dried, trim the ends of the braid by cutting blunt, flat tips (rather than angled tips), as this will make the clasp ends hold and grip the cords more securely. No more than 1in (2.5cm) should be cut off the ends.

7 Apply a fresh coat of thread glue to one end of the braid and insert it into one side of the magnetic clasp. Hold it firmly in place for about 30 seconds.

8 Repeat Step 7 with the other side of both the leather braid and the magnetic clasp. Leave all coats of glue to dry completely before wearing the bracelet.

Semiprecious stones

Integrating gemstones with jewelry not only adds a natural element, but can also create textural variations for any design. Like metals, gemstones come in many different kinds with their values based on several factors. Rarity and variety carry the most weight in determining how valuable a stone can be. Most gemstone components receive a variety of cuts and polishes that help enhance the stone's color and hue, while some stones, like agate, are dyed to produce a completely different shade. Fortunately, these variations in physical properties and appearance result in giving you an incomparable selection of colors and patterns to choose from.

Hazel

ZE: *Adjustable, one size fits most*

pon first glance, labradorite stone appears to be a rather dull, uninteresting rock lored with shades of gray. However, in the presence of light, this unique gemstone oduces an extraordinary optical phenomenon (known as "schiller effect") where the ck's surface emits an iridescent glow of bright blue and green flashes. There's no oubt that this spectacular trait makes these tiny gemstone beads the clear focal piece f this bracelet!

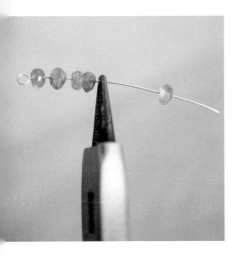

TOOLS AND MATERIALS

- 2in (5cm) 24-gauge gold-plated eyepin
- Seven 5mm labradorite rondelles
- Chain-nose pliers
- Wire cutters
- Round-nose pliers
- 1mm cotton embroidery thread in navy blue
- Ruler
- Scissors
- Clipboard
- Sticky tape
- Thread glue (or clear nail polish)

Take the eyepin and thread on all seven abradorite rondelles.

2 Using chain-nose pliers, bend the eyepin 90 degrees at the top of the last bead.

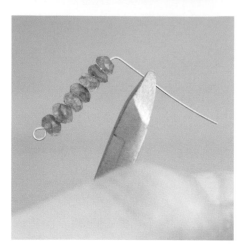

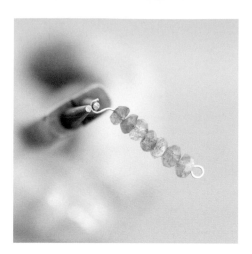

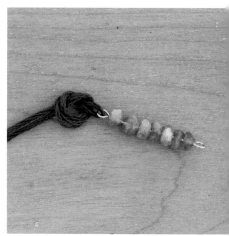

TIP

Be sure to hold the center of the beaded eyepin steady while forming the loop so that the pin remains straight and does not bend out of shape.

3 Using wire cutters, cut the pin about ¼in (6mm) after the last bead.

4 Grasp the very tip of the bent wire with the round-nose pliers. Rotate the pliers inward (without letting go of the wire tip) to form a complete loop, with the end of the wire touching the base of the loop.

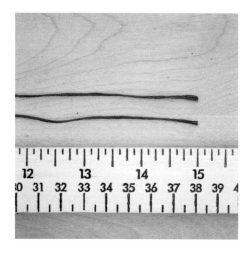

5 Next, cut five lengths of thread: two strands measuring 15in (38cm), which will be the base cords, two strands measuring 3ft (91cm), which will be the tying cords, and one strand measuring 7in (18cm).

6 Take one of the 15in (38cm) base cords and thread it through a loop on the beaded eyepin.

7 Fold the cord in half by bringing the ends together, and then tie an overhand knot at the base of the wire loop. Repeat Step 6 with the other side of the beaded pin, using the remaining 15in (38cm) base cord. You should have a beaded eyepin with two strands tied on each end loop.

Tape one side of the loose strands to the clipboard.

9 Take one of the 3ft (91cm) tying cords by the center and place it perpendicularly under the base cords. Tie an overhand knot around the base cords, just below the wire loop of the eyepin.

10 Using the square-knot macramé technique (see pp.16–18), make a braid 3in (7.5cm) long.

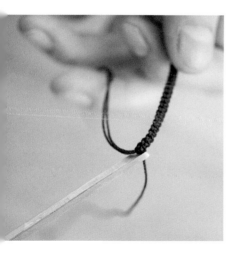

11 Close off the braid by making an overhand knot with the tying cords. Cut the excess strands of the tying cords and dab thread glue or clear nail polish on the knot to prevent it from unraveling.

12 Repeat Steps 9–11 with the base cords on the other side of the eyepin, using the remaining 3ft (91cm) tying cord. When finished, remove the cords from the clipboard.

13 Using the 7in (18cm) length of cord, make an adjustable pull-tie closure (see pp.19–20) to finish the bracelet.

Cameron

SIZE: 7in (18cm) bracelet

Agate is a popular gemstone used quite often in jewelry, mainly because of its colorful stripes and patterns. Actually, there's no gemstone that is as colorfully striped as agate. The incredible striping is a result of concentric layers (similar to rings of a tree trunk) formed by filling holes in volcanic rock or lava. Agate can be found in many amazing color variations—this particular number shows off a stunning green agate oval-shaped bead set between multiple strands of thin tan leather cords.

TOOLS AND MATERIALS

- 25mm green agate oval gemstone bead
- 1½in (4cm) gold-plated eyepin
- Chain-nose pliers
- Round-nose pliers
- 1mm round leather cord in tan
- Ruler
- Scissors
- 6mm gold-plated leather cord end
- Thread glue (or clear nail polish)
- Two 6mm gold-plated open jump rings
- Gold-plated lobster clasp

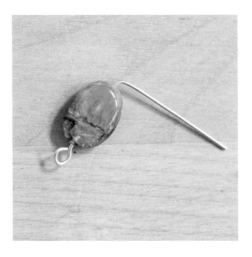

1 String the agate bead onto the eyepin and, using the chain-nose pliers, bend the pin 90 degrees at the top of the gemstone.

2 Grasp the very tip of the bent wire using the round-nose pliers, and then slowly rotate the pliers inward (without letting go of the wire tip) to form a complete loop, with the tip of the wire now touching the base of the loop. The agate bead should be strung on a pin with closed loops on either side.

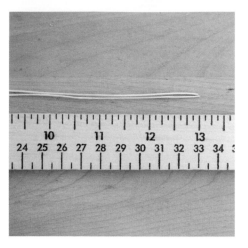

3 Next, cut two strands of the leather cord, both measuring 13in (33cm), and align the ends.

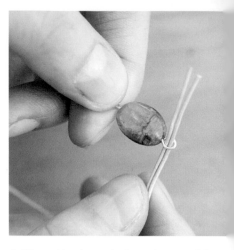

4 Thread both cords through one of the loops on the beaded eyepin.

5 Fold the cords in half by bringing both ends together and tie them to the loop by making an overhand knot. You should have four loose strands of leather cord tied onto the loop of the eyepin by a knot.

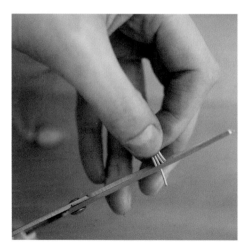

6 Trim the ends of the leather cords so that they are equal in length.

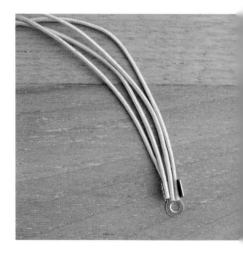

7 Bunch all four tips of the cords together and insert them into the foldover cord end, making sure the cords are straight and do not overlap each other or twist together.

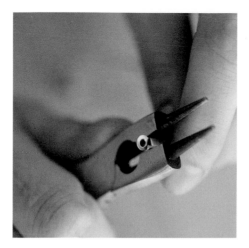

8 Using the chain-nose pliers, fold each side of the cord end by pinching them down over the leather cords.

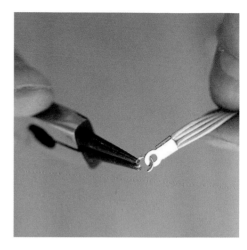

9 Slip an open jump ring onto the loop ring of the cord end, and then hook the lobster clasp onto the jump ring.

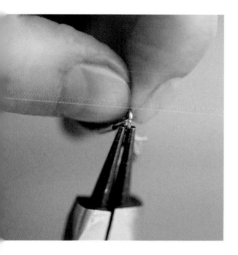

10 Close the jump ring by holding one side between your index finger and thumb, and with the other hand holding the chain-nose pliers, line up the seams of the ring.

11 Finally, attach the remaining jump ring to the other eyepin loop (on the other side of the bead).

12 Close the jump ring. Use the lobster clasp to hook onto the closed ring to fasten on the bracelet.

Ruby

SIZE: 7in (18cm) bracelet

Feminine and fun, this piece is perfect for those who love the delicate glitter of garnets. Cream-colored cotton cords pair up with the ruby red shade from the garnet gemstone rondelles to create this stunning, romance-inspired piece. Each garnet bead is hand strung onto the cotton cords which are then braided using the three-stranded braid technique. Finish with a bright gold-plated button bead closure. Capturing bohemian chic flair, this design is so simple and almost effortless to make!

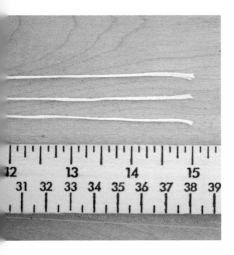

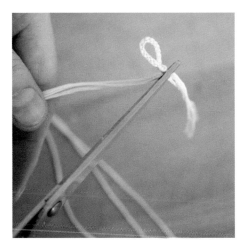

TOOLS AND MATERIALS

- 1mm cotton embroidery thread in cream
- Ruler
- Scissors
- 6mm gold disc button bead
- Thread glue (or clear nail polish)
- Clipboard
- Sticky tape
- 20–25 4mm garnet rondelle bead mix (beads range from 4–6mm)

1 Cut three strands of thread, each measuring 15in (38cm).

2 Line up the ends of all three cords and make a braided loop for the button bead closure (see p.21). Make sure the loop is slightly larger than the disc button bead—in this case, the loop should be about 3/8in (8–10mm). Trim any excess thread.

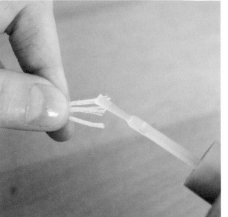

3 Take the other ends of the cords and dab the tips with thread glue or clear nail polish. Leave the glue to dry. The stiffened, glued ends will make it easier to thread the beads onto the cords and prevent the ends from fraying.

4 Once the glue has dried, secure the cords to the clipboard by taping down the button loop.

5 Using the three-stranded braid technique (see pp.14–15), make a tight braid about 1½in (4cm) long, then tie an overhand knot with all three cords.

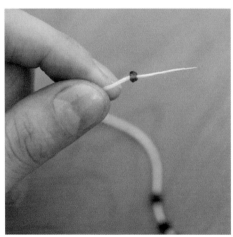

6 Then string 7–10 rondelle beads onto each of the three cords.

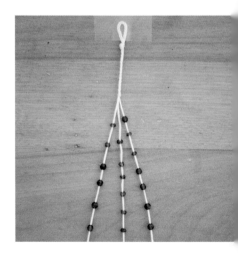

7 Once all the beads have been strung on, evenly space them apart on each cord, with about ¼in (6mm) between each bead. The distance from the first bead to the last should be roughly 2½–3in (5–7.5cm).

Loosely braid the beaded strands until ou come to the last bead. Tie an overhand not with all three cords.

9 Braid the rest of the cords another 1½in (4cm), as in Step 5, and finish by tying another overhand knot.

0 Thread on the disc button bead for the losure. Knot it, trim away excess strands, nd dab thread glue or clear nail polish on he knot to secure it and prevent it from oming undone.

Audrey

SIZE: 14in (35cm) bracelet

Charm jewelry will forever remain a classic favorite and a basic essential piece to any accessories collection. Perhaps it's because charms give us the opportunity to express ourselves through an endless variety of shapes, figures, symbols, and even words, all of which help to represent a significant sentiment of our lives. Or perhaps it's just the enjoyment of having a little shiny something sparkling with every movement we make. While most are made of metal, sometimes charms are made using gemstones—like this piece featuring tiny citrine, rose quartz, and lemon jade beads—that create a colorful show on our hands and wrists.

TOOLS AND MATERIALS

- About 20 x 6mm citrine, rose quartz, and lemon jade gemstone rondelles mix
- About 20 x 1in (2.5cm) gold-plated headpins (same quantity as bead mix)
- Chain-nose pliers
- Wire cutters
- Round-nose pliers
- 1mm cotton embroidery thread in tan
- Ruler
- Scissors
- Two 3mm gold-plated crimp ends
- Thread glue (or clear nail polish)
- Clipboard
- Sticky tape
- Two 6mm gold-plated open jump rings
- Gold-plated lobster clasp
- 6mm gold-plated closed jump ring

1 Gather the gemstone rondelles, headpins, and all three pliers to start making the gemstone charms. String a rondelle bead onto a headpin and bend the wire 90 degrees after the bead using chain-nose pliers.

2 Using wire cutters, cut a ¼in (6mm) off the end of the bent wire pin.

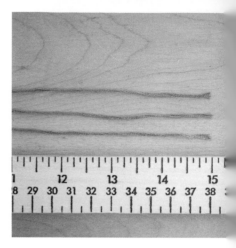

3 Next, grasp the very tip of the bent wire the round-nose pliers and slowly rotate the pliers inward (without letting go of the wire tip) to form a complete loop, with the tip of the wire now touching the top of the gemstone. You should have a small

gemstone bead sitting on top of the flat head of the headpin with a round loop ring on top of the bead. Repeat Steps 1–3 for each rondelle until all gemstone charms have been made.

4 Cut three equal lengths of tan embroidery thread, each measuring 15in (38cm).

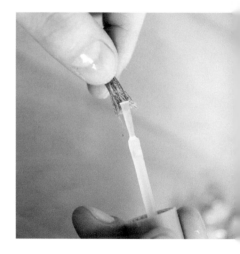

5 Align the ends of all three cords and insert the tips into a crimp end. Add a drop of thread glue or clear nail polish to the inserted cord tips for extra hold.

6 Using the chain-nose pliers, fold both sides of the crimp end by pinching each one down over the cords. You should have three loose strands with one capped end and the other unfinished.

7 Dab the tips of the unfinished side on all three cords with thread glue and leave the glue to dry. The stiffened, glued ends will make it easier to thread the cords through the loop rings of the gemstone charms.

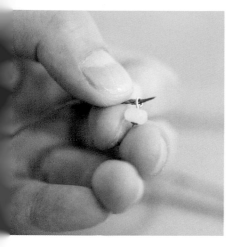

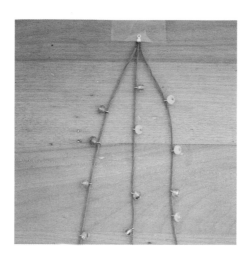

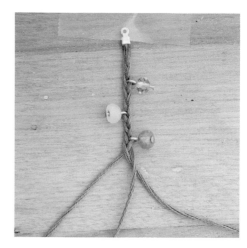

Randomly string the charms onto the cord strands by threading each cord through the headpin loop, with approximately 5 to 6 beads per strand. Tie a loose overhand knot at the end of each cord to prevent the charms from falling off while braiding.

9 Secure the beaded cords to the clipboard by taping down the capped end. Lay the clipboard on a flat horizontal surface and spread the charms evenly along each cord.

10 With the clipboard still lying flat, use the three-stranded braid technique (see pp.14–15) to braid the entire length of the cords. Make the braid fairly tight to keep the charms in place.

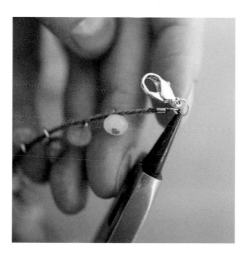

11 Hold the end of the braid to prevent it from unraveling and remove the cords from the clipboard. Insert the cord tips into the remaining crimp end, add a drop of glue to the tips inside the crimp, and use the chain-nose pliers to fold down the sides of the crimp.

12 Slip an open jump ring onto a crimp end loop and hook the lobster clasp onto the jump ring. Close the jump ring by holding one side between your index finger and thumb, and with the other hand holding the chain-nose pliers, line up the seams of the ring.

13 Repeat Step 12 using the remaining open jump ring on the other crimp end of the braided cords, replacing the lobster clasp with the closed jump ring. Use the lobster clasp to hook onto the closed ring to fasten on the bracelet.

Corinne

SIZE: 14in (35cm) bracelet

Capturing a true "boho" essence, this piece brings us back to Mother Nature with its use of earthy gemstones. From vibrant turquoise to the subtle agate, there's a plethora of colors and shades woven into the macramé braid, especially with this double-wrapped design! Close off the bracelet with a shiny gold disc bead—a perfect complement to contrast the subdued neutral tones.

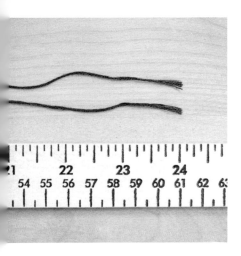

1 Cut three lengths of thread: one length measuring 2ft (61cm) and two lengths measuring 5ft (1.5m).

2 Line up the ends of all three cords and make a braided loop for the button bead closure (see p.21). Make sure the loop is slightly larger than the disc button bead—in this case, the loop should be about 3/8in (8–10mm). Trim any excess thread. You now have a braided button clasp loop with one short strand and two longer ones.

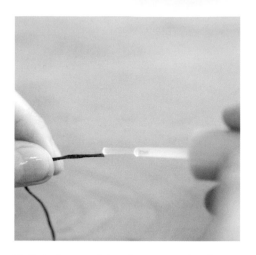

3 Dab the tip of the shortest cord with thread glue or clear nail polish. Leave the glue to dry. The stiffened, glued end will make it easier to thread the beads onto the cord and prevent the end from fraying.

4 String 30–40 beads onto the short strand, using your own judgment as to the arrangement of bead types and colors. Then tie a loose overhand knot at the end of the strand to prevent the beads from falling off while braiding.

5 Secure the cords to the clipboard by taping down the button loop. Arrange the cords so that the beaded strand is between the two longer strands. The beaded strand will be the base cord and the longer outer strands will be the tying cords.

6 Using the square-knot macramé technique (see pp.16–18), make a ½in (1.2cm) braid—about four full square knots.

7 Slide the first bead all the way up so that it sits below the braid, then make the first half of a square knot, tightening the tying cords around the bead.

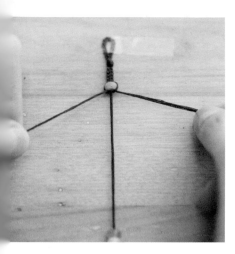

Make the second half of the square knot complete the full square knot.

9 Next, bring the second bead up and repeat Steps 7 and 8. Continue until all beads have been braided on. Make sure that a full square knot has been completed after every bead. You should end up with a 12in (30cm) long beaded macramé braid.

10 Finish the end by making four full square knots, as in Step 6, then tie an overhand knot with all three cords.

11 String on the disc button bead for the closure. Knot it, trim excess strands, and dab thread glue to secure the knot and prevent it from coming undone.

Naomi

SIZE: Adjustable, one size fits most

Although quartz gemstones are the most commonly found natural crystalline minerals on Earth, cherry quartz is actually a man-made rock that is dyed in very pretty shades of bright pink. Despite its origins, the stunningly vibrant pink hue is the reason why this gemstone remains a popular favorite. Cherry quartz gemstones range from light strawberry pink to a rich fuchsia color, like the beads used in this project. Braided onto bright teal cotton cords, this piece is for anyone who loves to show off some color!

TOOLS AND MATERIALS

- 1mm cotton embroidery thread in teal green
- Ruler
- Scissors
- Thread glue (or clear nail polish)
- Seven 6mm faceted cherry quartz beads
- Clipboard
- Sticky tape

1 Cut four lengths of thread: one strand measuring 15in (38cm), which will be the base cord, two strands measuring 3ft (91cm), which will be the tying cords, and one strand measuring 7in (18cm).

2 Line up the ends of all three cords and tie an overhand knot about 3in (7.5cm) from the end. You should end up with three strands all measuring 3in (7.5cm) on one side of the knot, with two long tying cords and one shorter base cord on the other side of the knot.

3 Apply thread glue or clear nail polish to the tip of the shortest strand (the base cord). Leave the glue to dry. The stiffened, glued end will make it easier to thread the beads onto the cord and prevent it from fraying.

4 Begin stringing the cherry quartz beads onto the short strand. After the last bead is on, tie a loose overhand knot at the end of the cord to keep the beads from falling off.

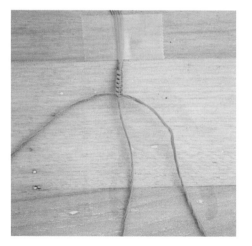

5 Secure the cords to the clipboard by taping down the 3in (7.5cm) loose ends. Separate the strands, arranging them so that the beaded base cord is in between the two long tying cords.

6 Using the square-knot macramé technique (see pp.16–18), make a ½in (1.2cm) braid—about six full square knots.

7 Slide the first bead all the way up so that it sits below the braid.

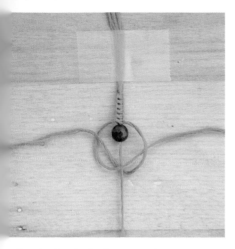

Tie the first half of a square knot, tightening the tying cords around the bead. Then tie the second half to complete the square knot.

9 Next, make another ½in (1.2cm) macramé braid. Slide the second bead up to the bottom of the braid.

10 Repeat Steps 8 and 9 until all the beads have been braided on. Make the final ½in (1.2cm) macramé braid and remove the cords from the clipboard.

1 Tie an overhand knot with all three strands.

12 Trim the strands, leaving about 4in (10cm) after the braid. Dab thread glue on the knot to keep it from coming undone.

13 Using the 7in (18cm) length of cord, make an adjustable pull-tie closure (see pp.19–20) to finish the bracelet.

Kiera

SIZE: Adjustable, one size fits most

A popular gemstone most notably sourced in China, jade is quite often used to create intricate ornaments, shapes, or sculptures, in addition to being used for jewelry components. Along with its rich color variations of greens, blues, and pinks, the ability to easily carve and sculpt this gem is what makes jade so appealing and versatile. This simple piece features a round, donut-shaped jade stone in a pale, light green shade set between matching olive-colored cords in a macramé braid.

TOOLS AND MATERIALS

- 1mm cotton embroidery thread in olive green
- Ruler
- Scissors
- 10mm light green jade donut bead
- Clipboard
- Sticky tape
- Thread glue (or clear nail polish)

1 Cut five lengths of thread: two strands measuring 15in (38cm), which will be the base cords, two strands measuring 3ft (91cm), which will be the tying cords, and one strand measuring 7in (18cm).

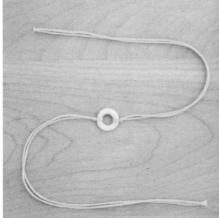

2 Tie one of the 15in (38cm) cords onto the donut bead by stringing one end through the hole and tying an overhand knot at the cord center. Repeat on the other side, using the remaining 15in (38cm) cord.

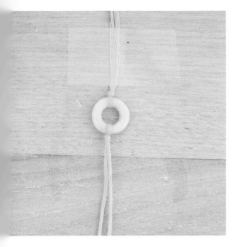

Secure the cords and bead to the clipboard by taping down one side of the base cords.

4 Take one of the 3ft (91cm) cords by the center and place it perpendicularly under the base cords. Tie an overhand knot around the base cords, just below the donut bead.

5 Using the square-knot macramé technique (see pp.16–18), make a braid 2½in (6.5cm) long.

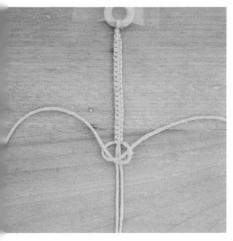

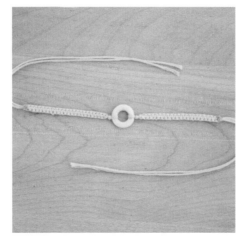

6 Then tie an overhand knot with just the tying cords to close off the braid. Trim the excess strands of the tying cords and dab thread glue or clear nail polish on the knot to prevent it from coming undone.

7 Remove the cords from the clipboard, tape down the braided side of the cords, and repeat Steps 4–6 using the remaining tying cord.

8 Using the 7in (18cm) length of cord, make an adjustable pull-tie closure (see pp.19–20) to finish the bracelet.

Diana

elonging to the quartz gemstone family, amethyst is one of the most precious and valuable minerals of this group. It is best distinguished by its radiant violet and purple ues—the darker the shade, the more valuable the stone. Amethyst can be carved quite easily into amazingly detailed ornaments. In this project, a polished amethyst ead in the shape of a heart sits as the focal piece, while a blend of blush pink and n cords surround the stone to complement and enhance the violet color variations.

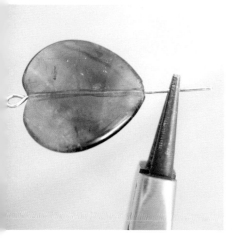

TOOLS AND MATERIALS

- 25mm heart-shaped amethyst bead
- 1½in (4cm) gold-plated eyepin
- Chain-nose pliers
- Round-nose pliers
- 1mm cotton embroidery thread in blush pink
- 1mm cotton embroidery thread in tan
- Ruler
- Scissors
- Clipboard
- Sticky tape
- Thread glue (or clear nail polish)

String the heart-shaped bead onto he eyepin and, using chain-nose pliers, end the pin 90 degrees at the top of he gemstone.

2 Grasp the very tip of the bent wire using round-nose pliers, and then slowly rotate the pliers inward (without letting go of the wire tip) to form a complete loop, with the tip of the wire now touching the base of the loop. The bead should now be strung on a pin with closed loops on either side.

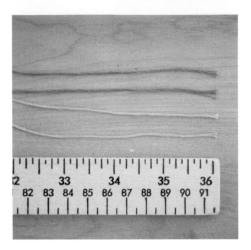

3 Cut three lengths of the blush pink thread, one strand measuring 15in (38cm), which will be the base cords, and two strands measuring 3ft (91cm), which will be the tying cords. Repeat with the tan thread.

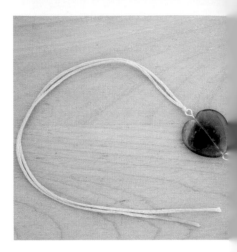

4 String the blush pink cord through one of the loops on the beaded eyepin. Then fold the cord in half by bringing both ends together and tie them to the wire loop by making an overhand knot.

5 Repeat Step 4 on the other side of the eyepin using the tan cord. You should have two loose strands in blush pink tied onto one eyepin loop (the blush pink base cords), and two strands in tan on the other eyepin loop (the tan base cords), with the heart in between.

6 Secure the cords to the clipboard by taping down one of the colored base cords.

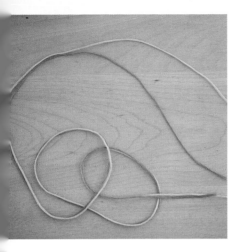

7 Now take one tan tying cord and one blush pink tying cord and bring them together to use as one strand. Make sure both cords are evenly aligned.

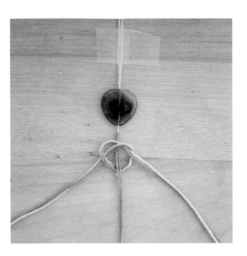

8 Take the combined tying cords by the center and place them perpendicularly under the base cords. Tie an overhand knot around the base cords, just below the eyepin loop.

9 Using the square-knot macramé technique (see pp.16–18), make a braid 2½in (6.5cm) long.

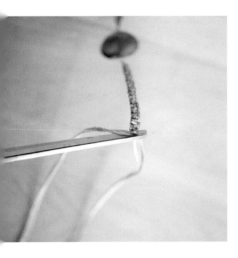

10 When finished, tie an overhand knot with only the tying cords to close off the braid. Trim the excess strands of the tying cords and dab thread glue or clear nail polish on the knot to keep it from coming undone.

11 Remove the cords from the clipboard, tape down the braided side, and repeat Steps 7–10. Afterward, you should have a wire-wrapped heart centered between two macramé braids in a blush pink–tan color mix.

12 To finish the bracelet, cut a 7in (18cm) piece of thread in your choice of blush or tan, and use it to make an adjustable pull-tie closure (see pp.19–20).

Crystals and glass

Being one of the most affordable and easily transformable materials on Earth, glass jewelry components come in all sorts of colors, shapes, and sizes. From simple seed beads to brilliantly cut crystals, no other material can compare to the unbelievable assortment of glass beads and components. While the Czech and Japanese are known for producing the best quality glass beads, there's no question as to who reigns in crystal-making. Although technically, crystals are simply a different (albeit better) type of glass, Austrian Swarovski crystals are undoubtedly in a class of their own. Every Swarovski-lover knows that there's nothing simple about a Swarovski crystal—a closer look reveals strikingly brilliant cuts and facets, both inside and out, making the piece shine bright like a diamond.

Paris

ith a seemingly endless variety of colors and components, there's never a shortage
 design options or ideas when it comes to using Swarovski crystals. Conveying a
ess is more" tone, this piece features an uncomplicated, straightforward rectangular
ystal bar set between subtle pale pink macramé braids. The component itself is
ctually a sew-on rhinestone with two open holes located on either side of the bar,
aking it easy to sew or link on to any project. And true to form, a closer look reveals
e brilliancy of Swarovski craftsmanship which gives the piece a remarkable shine.

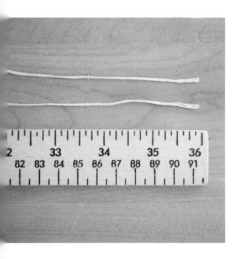

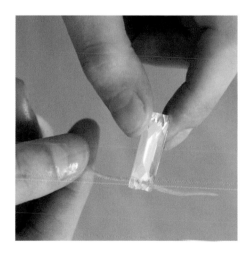

TOOLS AND MATERIALS

- 1mm cotton embroidery thread
  in light pink
- Ruler
- Scissors
- 6x24mm Swarovski Elements sew-on
  rhinestone crystal bar
- Clipboard
- Sticky tape
- Thread glue (or clear nail polish)

 Cut five lengths of thread: two strands
easuring 15in (38cm), which will be
he base cords, two strands measuring
ft (91cm), which will be the tying cords,
nd one strand measuring 7in (18cm).

2 Take a 15in (38cm) base cord and
thread it through one of the open holes
on the crystal bar.

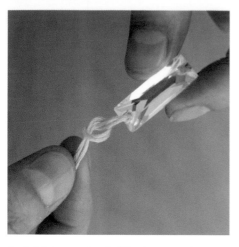

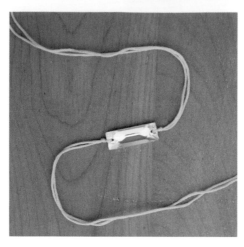

3 Fold the cord in half by bringing the ends together to make two strands, and then tie an overhand knot next to the hole.

4 Repeat Step 3 with the other side of the bar using the remaining base cord.

5 Tape down one side of the loose cords to the clipboard.

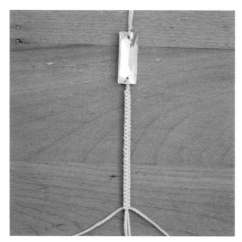

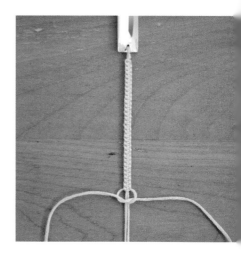

6 Take one of the 3ft (91cm) tying cord by the center and place it perpendicularly under the base cords. Tie an overhand knot around the base cords, just below the hole of the crystal bar.

7 Using the square-knot macramé technique (see pp.16–18), make a braid about 3in (7.5cm) long.

8 Close off the braid by making an overhand knot with the tying cords.

Cut the excess strands of the tying cords
d dab thread glue or clear nail polish on
e knot to prevent it from unraveling.

10 Remove the cords from the clipboard,
secure the other side, and repeat Steps
6–9 with the base cords on the other side
of the crystal bar, using the remaining 3ft
(91cm) tying cord. When finished, remove
the cords from the clipboard. You should
have about 4in (10cm) of loose strands on
each side of a 3in (7.5cm) macramé braid,
with the Swarovski crystal bar at the center.

11 Using the 7in (18cm) length of
cord, make an adjustable pull-tie closure
(see pp.19–20) to finish the bracelet.

(see pp.19–20)

TIP
....
*For pieces that use a slightly heavier
focal component, try making the braid
a little tighter. The tighter the braid, the
stiffer the bracelet, providing a sturdier
base to support the centerpiece.*

Jennifer

SIZE: 7in (18cm) bracelet

Glass seed beads are among the most popular and commonly used beads within the beading community. The plethora of different colors and sizes, available in a variety of cuts and finishes, make these beads extremely versatile and easy to incorporate into any project or design. This particular piece features tiny 2mm beads, in a stunning sapphire blue, that wrap all the way around the wrist. The beads' transparent finish gives the right amount of shine to bring the pale gray cords to life, while the hex-cut design creates a faceted surface that enhances the vibrant blue hues.

TOOLS AND MATERIALS

- 1mm cotton embroidery thread in light gray
- Ruler
- Scissors
- 6mm silver disc button bead
- Thread glue (or clear nail polish)
- 5g size 8/0 hex-cut transparent sapphire seed beads
- Clipboard
- Sticky tape

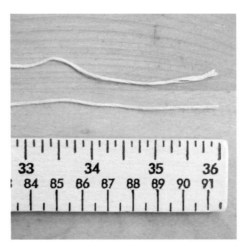

1 Cut three lengths of thread: one strand measuring 16in (40cm), which will be the beaded base cord, and two strands measuring 3ft (91cm), which will be the tying cords.

2 Line up the ends of all three cords and make a braided loop for the button bead closure (see p.21). Trim any excess thread. You now have a braided closure loop with one short strand and two longer ones.

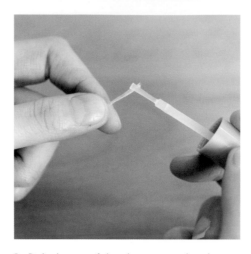

3 Dab the tip of the shortest cord with thread glue or clear nail polish. Leave the glue to dry. The stiffened, glued end will make it easier to thread the beads onto the cord and prevent the end from fraying.

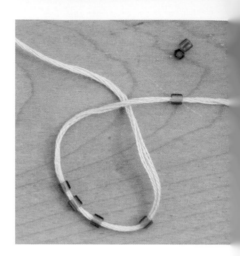

4 Once the glue has dried, begin stringing the seed beads onto the short strand. This project requires about 30 beads.

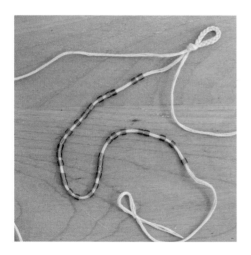

5 Tie a loose overhand knot at the end of the bead strand to prevent the beads from falling off while braiding.

6 Secure the cords to the clipboard by taping down the button loop. Arrange the cords so that the beaded strand (the base cord) is in the middle of the two longer strands (the tying cords).

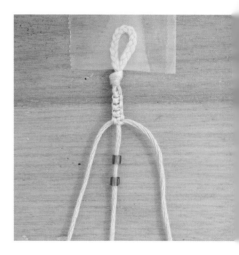

7 Using the square-knot macramé technique (see pp.16–18), make a braid ½in (1.2cm) long—about four or five full square knots.

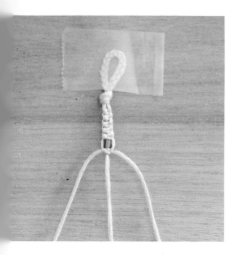

Next, slide the first seed bead all the way up so that it sits below the macramé braid. Make the first half of a square knot, tightening the tying cords around the bead.

9 Then make the second half of the square knot to complete the full knot. Bring the second bead up and repeat Steps 8 and 9.

10 Continue doing this until all beads have been braided on. Make sure a full square knot has been completed after every bead. The braided bead strand should measure about 5½in (14cm) to make a 7in (18cm) bracelet.

TIP
....
If the braided bead strand measures less than 5½in (14cm), braid on a few more beads until the desired length is reached. If the strand is longer than 5½in (14cm), remove a few beads by undoing the braid.

11 Finish the end by making four full square knots, as in Step 7, and then tie an overhand knot with all three cords.

12 String on the silver disc bead for the button closure. Knot it, trim off any excess cords, and dab thread glue to secure the knot and prevent it from coming undone.

Charlize

This sweet, dainty piece features a tiny single Swarovski crystal stone in a bezel-set channel link. The gold-plated setting creates a halo effect surrounding the sparkling crystal stone that gives the piece a classy, sophisticated look. With two open holes attached on either side of the bezel setting, this component can easily be linked to any stringing material. This project uses pale lilac-colored cotton cords in a macramé braid to create a pretty, feminine design perfect for springtime!

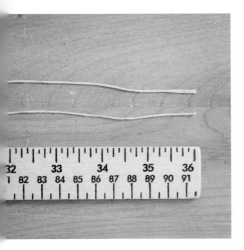

TOOLS AND MATERIALS

- 1mm cotton embroidery thread in lilac
- Ruler
- Scissors
- 6mm gold-plated Swarovski Elements crystal channel link
- Clipboard
- Sticky tape
- Thread glue (or clear nail polish)

1 Cut five lengths of thread: two strands measuring 15in (38cm), which will be the base cords, two strands measuring 3ft (91cm), which will be the tying cords, and one strand measuring 7in (18cm).

2 Take a 15in (38cm) base cord and thread it through one of the open holes on the crystal link.

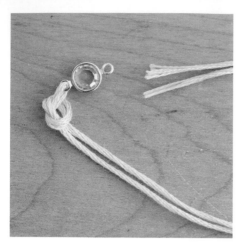

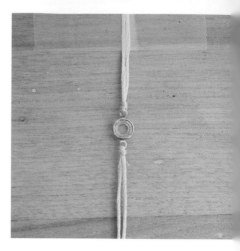

3 Fold the cord in half by bringing the ends together to make two strands, and then tie an overhand knot next to the hole.

4 Repeat Step 3 with the other side of the link, using the remaining base cord.

5 Tape down one side of the loose cords to the clipboard.

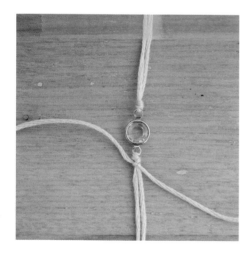

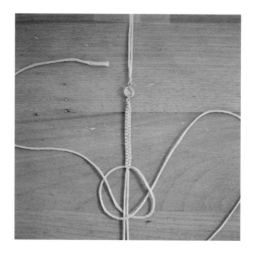

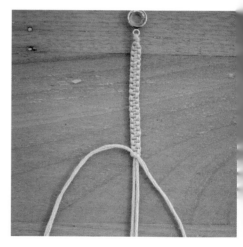

6 Then one of the 3ft (91cm) tying cord by the center and place it perpendicularly under the base cords. Tie an overhand knot around the base cords, just below the hole of the channel link.

7 Using the square-knot macramé technique (see pp.16–18), make a braid about 3in (7.5cm) long.

8 Close off the braid by making an overhand knot with the tying cords.

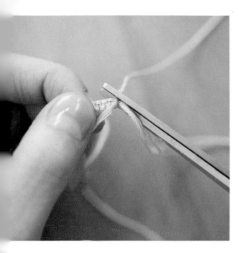 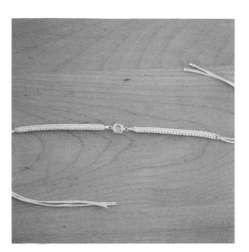 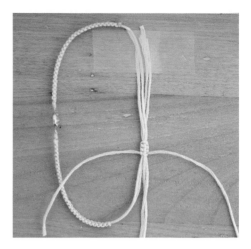

Cut the excess strands of the tying cords nd dab thread glue or clear nail polish on he knot to prevent it from unraveling.

10 Remove the cords from the clipboard, secure the other side, and repeat Steps 6–9 with the base cords on the other side of the link, using the remaining 3ft (91cm) tying cord. When finished, remove the cords from the clipboard. You should have about 4in (10cm) of loose strands on each side of a 3in (7.5cm) macramé braid, with the crystal channel link at the center.

11 Using the 7in (18cm) length of cord, make an adjustable pull-tie closure (see pp.19–20) to finish the bracelet.

Nicole

SIZE: 7in (18cm) bracelet

When it comes to stackable jewelry, the thing that's most appealing is the ability to customize the pieces by mixing and matching different designs for a look that's uniquely your own. Part of that fun includes creating a palette of your favorite colors in the brightest, most vibrant shades you can find. But every rainbow needs that occasional neutral component to complement the bright tones and help create a balanced look—and that's just what this project brings. From cream-colored cotton cords to crystal clear beads, this neutral piece is perfect for stacking with any dizzying array of bold hues... or for anyone who prefers the straightforward clean simplicity of white on white.

TOOLS AND MATERIALS

- 1mm cotton embroidery thread in cream
- Ruler
- Scissors
- Thread glue (or clear nail polish)
- Clipboard
- Sticky tape
- Six 6mm crystal Swarovski Elements round beads

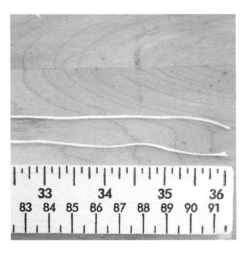

1 Cut three lengths of thread: one strand measuring 16in (40cm), which will be the base cord, and two strands measuring 3ft (91cm), which will be the tying cords.

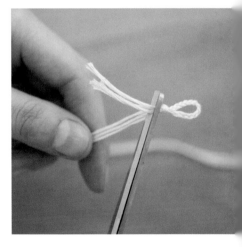

2 Line up the ends of all three cords and make a braided loop for the button bead closure. Here, we are using one of the crystals for the closure. Make sure the loop is slightly larger than the crystal—in this case, the loop should be about 3/8in (8–10mm). Trim any excess thread.

3 Apply thread glue or clear nail polish to the tip of the shortest strand. Leave the glue to dry. The stiffened, glued end will make it easier to thread the beads onto the cord and prevent it from fraying.

4 Secure the cords to the clipboard by taping down the button loop. Separate the strands, arranging them so that the shortest cord (the base cord) is in between the two long ones (the tying cords).

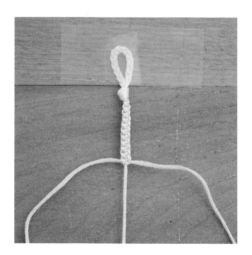

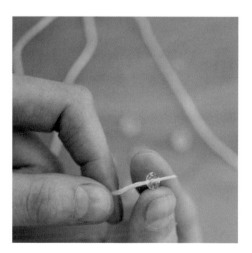

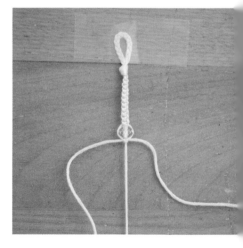

5 Using the square-knot macramé technique (see pp.16–18), make a braid 1in (2.5cm) long—about 12 full square knots.

6 String a crystal bead onto the base cord and slide it all the way up so that it sits below the braid.

7 Tie the first half of a square knot, tightening the tying cords around the bead. Then tie the second half to complete the square knot. Make six more full square knots (about ½in/1.2cm macramé braid).

8 String on another crystal bead, bringing it all the way up to the bottom of the last ½in (1.2cm) braid.

9 Repeat Steps 7 and 8 until a total of six beads have been braided on.

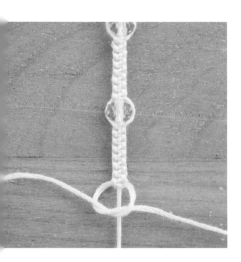

10 Make one last ½in (1.2cm) macramé braid, then remove the cords from the clipboard.

11 Tie an overhand knot at the end of the braid using all three strands.

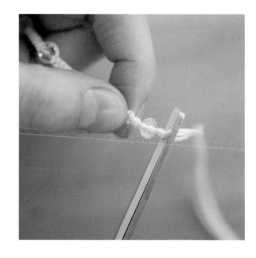

12 Finally, string the last crystal bead onto all three cords and secure it with another overhand knot. Trim excess strands and dab thread glue on the knot to keep it from coming undone.

Marilyn

SIZE: Adjustable, one size fits most

Although Shamballa bracelets have been around for centuries, it's only been in the past two years that they've become a trend in the fashion world. Originating from Tibet, these bracelets were used to help in meditative prayer, similar in purpose to Catholic rosary beads, and could be made using wooden, clay, or even diamond beads. However, today's inspiration of this outdated piece is most often found using pavé crystal beads. With tiny, sparkling crystal stones inlaid throughout the surface, there's no question as to how these beads brought an ancient style back to life. But this rendition utilizes petite 6mm beads, rather than the traditional 10mm, to create a dainty, modern twist on a show-stopping trend.

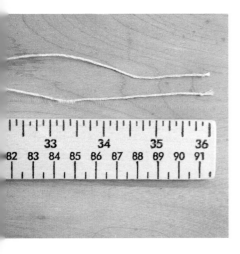

TOOLS AND MATERIALS

- 1mm cotton embroidery thread in light gray
- Silver metallic polyester thread
- Ruler
- Scissors
- Thread glue (or clear nail polish)
- Clipboard
- Sticky tape
- Ten 6mm pavé crystal beads in light rose

1 Cut three lengths of the light gray thread: one strand measuring 16in (40cm) and two strands measuring 3ft (91cm). Then cut the same quantity and lengths using the silver metallic thread.

2 Pair each strand of the metallic thread with a light gray cotton cord of matching length. Each metallic/gray cord duo will be used and considered as one strand throughout braiding.

3 Line up the ends of all three cords and tie an overhand knot about 4in (10cm) from the end. You should have a knot with loose 4in (10cm) strands on one side, while the other side has two long strands (the tying cords) and one short strand (the base cord).

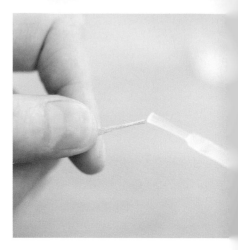

4 Apply thread glue or clear nail polish to the tip of the base cord and let dry. The stiffened, glued end will make it easier to thread the beads onto the cord and also prevent it from fraying.

5 Secure the cords to the clipboard by taping down the 4in (10cm) loose ends. Separate the strands by placing the short base cord in between the two longer tying cords.

6 Using the square-knot macramé technique (see pp.16–18), make a braid 1½in (4cm) long.

7 Next, string all ten pavé crystal beads onto the base cord and tie a loose overhand knot to prevent the beads from falling off while braiding.

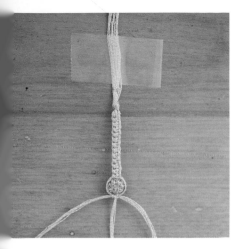

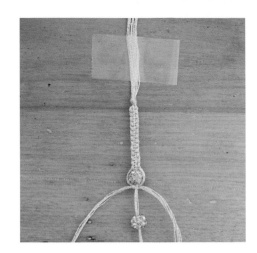

8 Slide the first bead all the way up to so that it sits below the braid. Make the first half of a square knot, tightening the tying cords around the bead. Then make the second half of the square knot.

9 Repeat Step 8 with the rest of the beads, making sure to complete a full square knot after each bead and before sliding the next one up.

10 After all beads have been woven on, make another 1½in (4cm) macramé braid. You should have ten pavé crystal beads braided and centered between 1½in (4cm) macramé braids on either side.

11 Close off the braid by tying an overhand knot with all three strands. Measure 4in (10cm) after the knot to use for the pull-tie closure and trim. Dab thread glue on the knot to prevent it from coming undone.

12 To finish the bracelet, cut a 7in (18cm) piece of gray thread and use it to make an adjustable pull-tie closure (see pp.19–20).

Fleur

SIZE: Adjustable, one size fits most

It's no secret that beads come in a vast variety of shapes, colors, and sizes. And with such a selection at our disposal, creating different designs and patterns couldn't be easier. Using a particular combination of bead colors and strategic placement can easily turn nothing into something! Take this project, for example: by aligning a couple beads, more or less, into three rows, all of a sudden we've designed a pattern in the shape of a pretty flower. Go more in depth by specifically using crystal beads in a pale transparent yellow (with a single clear bead for the center) and you've got yourself a sparkly little daisy.

TOOLS AND MATERIALS

- 1mm cotton embroidery thread in mint green
- Ruler
- Scissors
- Thread glue (or clear nail polish)
- Clipboard
- Sticky tape
- Six 4mm light yellow Swarovski Elements crystal round beads
- 6mm Swarovski Elements clear crystal bead

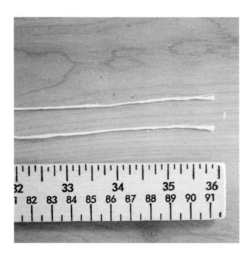

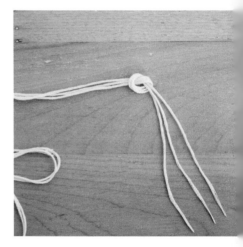

1 Cut four lengths of thread: one strand measuring 16in (40cm), which will be the base cords, two strands measuring 3ft (91cm), which will be the tying cords, and one strand measuring 7in (18cm).

2 Line up the ends of all three cords and tie an overhand knot about 3in (7.5cm) from the end. You should end up with three strands all measuring 3in (7.5cm) on one side of the knot, with two long tying cords and one shorter base cord on the other side of the knot.

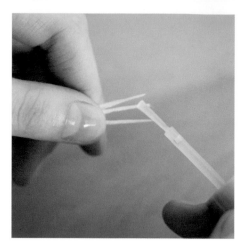

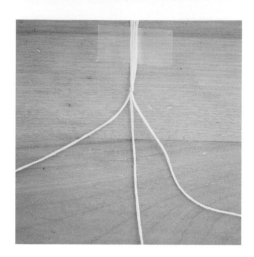

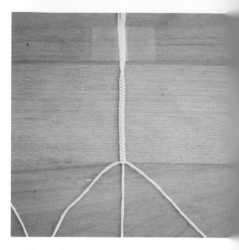

3 Apply thread glue or clear nail polish to the tips of all three strands on the uneven side. Leave the glue to dry. The stiffened, glued ends will make it easier to thread the beads onto the cords and prevent them from fraying.

4 Secure the cords to the clipboard by taping down the 3in (7.5cm) loose ends. Separate the strands by arranging the shortest cord (the base cord) in between the two longer ones (the tying cords).

5 Using the square-knot macramé techniqu (see pp.16–18), make a braid about 2.5in (5cm) long.

7 With the base cord, string on one yellow bead, one clear bead, and one yellow bead. Tie a loose overhand knot at the end of the cord to keep the beads from falling off. You should have three columns of beads: yellow–yellow on the left tying cord, yellow–clear–yellow on the base cord, and yellow–yellow on the right tying cord.

6 String two yellow crystal beads onto each tying cord. Tie loose overhand knots on the ends of the cords to prevent the beads from falling off.

TIP

If the flower looks misshapen or unsymmetrical after the full square knot is made, stop and reposition any bead that looks out of place. To check if your flower is shaped correctly, place it on a flat surface and bend down at eye level—all the beads should be evenly level and there should not be any sticking up or out. Ultimately, the bead shape of the daisy pattern should always be an equilateral hexagon.

Push all the beads on each cord all the way up to the bottom of the macramé braid, with the first yellow bead on the base cord actually touching the braid.

9 Tie the first half of a square knot, tightly wrapping each side of the three center beads with the two yellow beads on the tying cords. Tighten the tying cords around the base cord beads so that the outline of the beads creates a hexagonal shape. Make the second half of the square knot.

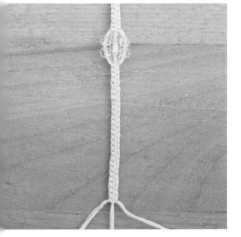

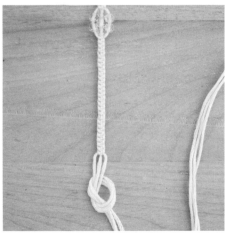
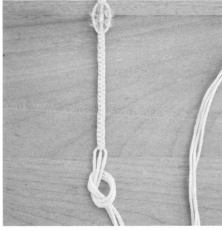

10 Make another 2.5in (5cm) macramé braid. You should have a crystal-bead daisy centered between 2.5in (5cm) macramé braids on either side.

11 Close off the braid by tying an overhand knot with all three cords. Measure 4in (10cm) after the knot to use for the pull-tie closure and trim. Dab thread glue on the knot to keep it from coming undone.

12 Using the 7in (18cm) length of cord, make an adjustable pull-tie closure (see pp.19–20) to finish the bracelet.

Julia

SIZE: 20in (50cm) bracelet

Most often used for pearl knotting, silk cords provide an alternative choice to your basic, everyday cotton embroidery floss. Strung onto luxurious light pink, triple-wrapped cords is a brilliant Swarovski crystal square button in a soft shade of violet. Foil backing is affixed to the underside of the button that produces a mirror effect to reflect and highlight the faceted cuts of the crystal—this famous Swarovski technique is what makes their crystals sparkle the brightest!

TOOLS AND MATERIALS

- Light pink no.16 (1.05mm) Griffin silk bead cord with attached needle
- Clothes iron or hair-straightening iron
- 10mm light amethyst Swarovski Elements crystal square button
- Ruler
- Thread glue (or clear nail polish)
- Scissors
- Two 3mm silver-plated crimp ends
- Chain-nose pliers
- Two 6mm silver-plated open jump rings
- 6mm silver-plated closed jump ring

1 To prepare the silk cord for use, you must first remove the kinks in the thread (a result of being wrapped around a thread card from packaging). To make the silk thread smooth and even, iron out the kinks using a clothes iron on the lowest setting (or the silk pre-set). Alternatively, a hair-straightening iron or curling iron can also be used. Make sure to use the lowest setting, and never keep the cord against the hot iron for more than 5 seconds.

2 Using the attached beading needle, thread the crystal button onto the cord by weaving the needle through the button holes. Start from the bottom foiled side of the button and pull the needle and cord through the first hole to the top faceted side.

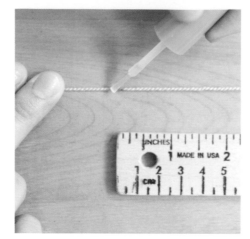

3 Then thread the needle through the second hole by bringing the cord back to the underside. The top of the button should have a strand of silk cord going across the center with both ends of the cord hanging from the underside.

4 Measure the cord at 20in (50cm), and mark the lengths by dabbing thread glue or clear nail polish to the 0in (0cm) and 20in (50cm) spots. Because silk cord is so soft and the thread is actually twisted together,

cutting the cord will cause it to fray and begin unraveling rather quickly. The glued marks on the cord help hold the cut cord together and keep it from unraveling long enough to attach the crimp ends.

TIP

Use your own preference on where you would like the button to be situated along the cord—you can always adjust its position later by sliding the button along the cord. But always pull the cord through one button hole at a time and never by making the cord slide through two holes at once, as this will cause the silk to fray.

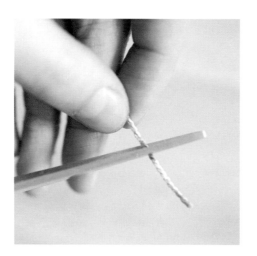

5 Once the glued spots have fully dried, take a pair of scissors to one end of the silk cord and cut down the middle of the glued area. Do not trim the other end until the first cut side is securely closed off with a crimp end.

6 Insert the cut tip into a crimp end and, using chain-nose pliers, fold down the sides of the crimp over the top of the cord.

7 Repeat Steps 5 and 6 with the other end of the cord. You should have a long silk cord with crimp ends attached on either side and the crystal button threaded somewhere along the strand.

8 Next, slip an open jump ring onto the loop of one of the crimp ends. Before closing it, slip the closed jump ring onto the open one. The closed jump ring will be the fastening loop for the lobster clasp.

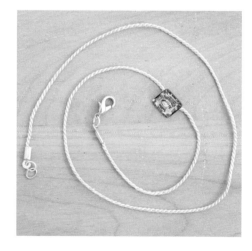

9 Close the open ring by holding one side between your index finger and thumb, and with the other hand holding the chain-nose pliers, line up the seams of the ring.

10 Slip the remaining open jump ring onto the loop on the other cord end, and then hook the lobster clasp onto the open jump ring.

11 Finally, close the ring by holding one side between your index finger and thumb, and with the other hand holding the chain-nose pliers, line up the seams of the ring to finish the bracelet.

Kate

SIZE: Adjustable, one size fits most

Crystal rhinestone chains are a favorite embellishment for crafters and jewelers everywhere. Honestly, who can resist sparkly strands of crystal shine? Unfortunately, these gorgeous chains can be quite tricky to work with, as they have no holes or loops for attachment, and affixing links, rings, or any jewelry finding becomes a daunting task. Thankfully, a neat little component called a chain crimp end can be attached to the chain via tiny prongs that hold it in place, while a small ring on the other side allows the chain to be linked to anything you want!

TOOLS AND MATERIALS

- 1mm cotton embroidery thread in lemon yellow
- Ruler
- Scissors
- Two 3mm gold-plated rhinestone chain crimp ends
- 2in (5cm) of 2.5mm Swarovski Elements gold-plated crystal rhinestone chain
- Chain-nose pliers
- Clipboard
- Sticky tape
- Thread glue (or clear nail polish)

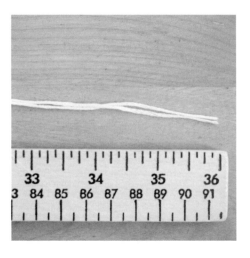

1 Cut five lengths of thread: two strands measuring 15in (38cm), which will be the base cords, two strands measuring 3ft (91cm), which will be the tying cords, and one strand measuring 7in (18cm).

2 Take a crimp end and place the last stone on the chain inside the crimp end.

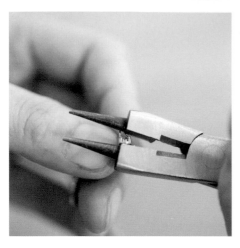

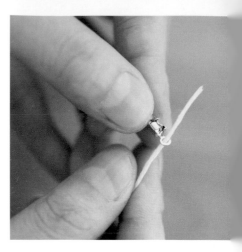

TIP

When folding down the prongs of the crimp end, use one hand to hold the crimp by the open ring while the other hand holds the chain-nose pliers.

3 Using chain-nose pliers, carefully bend and fold the prongs down over the top of the stone. Repeat on the other side of the chain using the remaining crimp end.

4 Take a 15in (38cm) base cord and thread it through the ring of one of the chain ends.

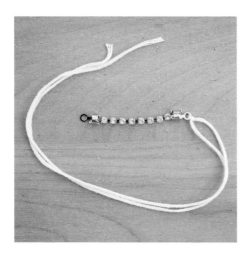

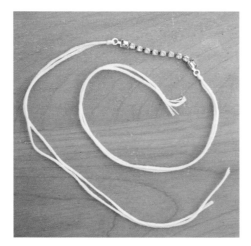

5 Fold the cord in half by bringing the ends together to make two strands, and then tie an overhand knot on the ring.

6 Repeat Steps 4 and 5 with the other side of the chain, using the remaining base cord. Then tape down one side of the loose strands to the clipboard.

7 Take one of the 3ft (91cm) tying cord by the center and place it perpendicularly under the base cords. Tie an overhand knot around the base cords, just below the ring on the chain end.

8 Using the square-knot macramé technique (see pp.16–18), make a braid in (5cm) long.

9 Close off the braid by making an overhand knot with the tying cords. Cut the excess strands of the tying cords and dab thread glue or clear nail polish on the knot to prevent it from unraveling.

10 Remove the cords from the clipboard, secure the other side, and repeat Steps 7–9 with the base cords on the other side of the chain, using the remaining 3ft (91cm) tying cord.

11 When finished, remove the cords from the clipboard. You should have loose strand ends from the base cords and a 2in (5cm) macramé braid on each side, with the crystal rhinestone chain at the center.

12 Using the 7in (18cm) length of cord, make an adjustable pull-tie closure (see pp.19–20) to finish the bracelet.

Index

Page numbers in bold refer to illustrations.

About the author

Born from a long line of artists and designers, Di Kim is no stranger to the world of creative art. Combining her love of fashion and style with a Do-It-Yourself mantra, this self-taught jewelry designer began creating pieces from her home in Houston, Texas. With a newfound respect for the creative arts, Di draws inspiration from her everyday life. While her design style conveys a minimalist nature of more contemporary and modern elements, she has genuine admiration for the sheer talent characterized by many amazing artists and designers, past and present. Di sells her jewelry online through Etsy, as well as at local boutiques and trade shows, and has successfully developed a loyal following.

Resources

Artbeads
Swarovski Elements, gemstones, sterling silver, beads, findings
www.artbeads.com

Auntie's Beads
Specialty beads, metal beads, glass and seed beads, pendants, charms, findings
www.auntiesbeads.com

Baubles & Beads
Beads, pearls, crystals and glass, chains and stringing materials, findings
www.baublesandbeads.com

Beadaholique
Swarovski Elements, beads, pendants and charms, stampings, jewelry chain, findings
www.beadaholique.com

Bead Trust
Beads: gemstones, glass, natural, pearls, and metal
www.beadtrust.com

Brightlings Beads
Crystal beads, gemstones, Bali silver beads, jewelry chain, findings, bead tools
www.brightlingsbeads.com

Fire Mountain Gems and Beads
Beads, gemstones, jewelry supplies and findings, stringing materials
www.firemountaingems.com

Hobby Lobby
Arts, crafts, jewelry-making, scrapbooking, home décor, floral, fabric
www.hobbylobby.com

Jewelry Supply
Jewelry findings, beads, Swarovski Elements crystals, jewelry displays and supplies
www.jewelrysupply.com

Michael's
General crafts, beads, art supplies, floral, scrapbooking, needle art
www.michaels.com

Monster Slayer
Glass beads, gemstones, jewelry findings, metal sheet and wire, metal-working tools
www.monsterslayer.com

Rings & Things
Beads, gemstones, findings, chains, stringing materials
www.rings-things.com

Rio Grande
Beads, gemstones, findings, stringing materials, jewelry tools and equipment
www.riogrande.com